PUPPYLOPAEDIA

A Complete Guide To Puppy Care

J.M. Evans
with Caroline Ackroyd-Gibson

RINGPRESS

THE QUESTION OF GENDER

The 'he' pronoun is used throughout this book in favour of the rather impersonal 'it', but no gender bias is intended.

Published by Ringpress Books,
A Division of Interpet Publishing
Vincent Lane, Dorking, Surrey RH4 3YX

ISBN 1 86054 239 5

Printed in Singapore

10 9 8 7 6 5 4 3 2 1

CONTENTS

(Naming your dog; Basic rules and tips; Cars; People; Other animals; Handling and grooming; Grooming tips; Health checks); A dog's ambitions (Know your dog).

prevented by vaccination; Vaccination regimes (Primary vaccination; Booster vaccinations; Targeted vaccinations).

ACKNOWLEDGEMENTS

My grateful thanks go first to three special ladies without whose input and support this publication would not have seen the light of day.

First to Caroline Ackroyd-Gibson, who was responsible for stimulating me to come out of retirement and put pen to paper again. Her views as the experienced breeder of *Toraylac* Cavalier King Charles Spaniels were particularly helpful and pertinent when the content of this book was being discussed at its formative stage. Her ideas have helped, I think, to give balance to the text.

Secondly, it would be remiss of me not to acknowledge the American veterinary surgeon Vicky Voith, who first stimulated my interest in dog behaviour 25 years ago. Vicky was a pioneer in this field; she was 'into' this subject long before it became 'cool' as it is today.

Thirdly, I acknowledge with gratitude the continuing support given to me by my wife, Monica. She was largely responsible for bringing up our Dobermann bitch, Anna, the original *'ideal dog'*. Monica has been an unfailing source of constructive criticism, and, as an author's spouse, she has put up with endless discussions and periods of distraction on my part, without complaint. This is truly the very last book (but one) I shall write – I promise!

My grateful thanks go also to Susan E. Shaw, veterinary surgeon and Senior Lecturer at the Department of Clinical Veterinary Science, University of Bristol, for her help with the details relating to ecto- and endo-parasite infections, making it possible to give up-to-date advice in respect of dogs travelling overseas. Similarly my thanks go to Sarah Heath BVSc MRCVS, who, on behalf of the Association of Pet Behaviour Counsellors, has readily given advice regarding the latest theories and terminology in respect of dog behaviour.

Lastly, my thanks to the team at the creative and marketing consultancy *Market Square* for their encouragement, particularly to Sue Bailey who typed the many drafts and the final script against all odds.

My hope is that this book will lead to there being more *ideal dogs* in this country and that their owners will reap in full the very real benefits that dog ownership can bring.

Jim Evans

INTRODUCTION

In the last decade or so, life for dog owners has changed considerably. The once-common infectious diseases (canine distemper, infectious canine hepatitis, canine parvovirus infection, and leptospirosis) have all been virtually eliminated. This is due to the development of combined and more efficacious vaccines, as well as a better understanding of how – and, importantly, at what age – vaccines should be administered. As a result, nowadays, more dogs are destroyed each year because their behaviour is inappropriate or dangerous than as a result of infectious disease.

A contributing factor to this situation is that many more people have become less tolerant and are more inclined to complain about dogs. Some even consider litigation. Dogs that bark excessively, chase cars, or threaten people are now commonly a major cause of friction in the community.

Against this background it is important that dog owners do all they can to ensure that their pet fits snugly into society at large, to save embarrassment and possible conflict.

In the 1950s and 60s, militaristic-style dog trainers held sway, using techniques to 'beat' dogs into submission and teaching owners how to dominate their dogs by the use of punishment and the threat of punishment. In the 1970s this approach began to be questioned. The transposition of the simplistic model of wolf behaviour to pet dogs started to be challenged by more and more animal behaviourists.

A defining moment in the UK came in 1988, when the Association of Pet Behaviour Counsellors was formed. This led to the whole question of dog behaviour and its modification being studied afresh and with a new vigour. As a result, much has been learnt in recent years about dog behaviour and how dogs can be 'shaped' to meet today's requirements. Importantly too, the inherited instincts of dogs, which would be useful in the wild but inappropriate for today's way of life, can now be largely suppressed by the use of modern behaviour control methods.

TOWARDS AN *IDEAL DOG*

Provided that puppy owners are willing to learn some simple facts and principles, and apply them correctly and consistently, the ownership of an *ideal dog* becomes a realistic goal. Fundamental to that is the appreciation of the need for puppies to be properly habituated and socialised, and for training to begin when they are young; particularly when they are between three and 13 weeks of age – it is at this stage of life that they are at the height of their learning ability. Furthermore, starting early in life means that owners have a clean slate to work on; there is no need for bad habits to be unlearnt and replaced by acceptable behaviour.

SOURCES OF INFORMATION

The bookshops are full of literary works instructing owners how to raise puppies and modify the behaviour of adult dogs – a bewildering choice. Some books perpetuate the old myths, some go into such protracted scientific detail that the owners are often left more confused. Yet others just give details of individual problems that may or may not be pertinent to every owner.

In contrast, this book aims to educate owners about the important general principles relating to modern dog behaviour modification techniques. We will show how they can be used most effectively. Armed with this fundamental knowledge, most owners will be able to work out for themselves what action is best to take as their puppy progresses.

FLEXIBLE MANAGEMENT

Puppies are not clones. Like children, they learn and mature at different rates. Some pups are extroverts, some are introverts, some are pushy, and some are fearful. Educating pups by rote is not a valid option. Our methodology brings with it the all-important flexibility of management that is necessary in raising and training puppies.

PREVENTING INAPPROPRIATE BEHAVIOUR

In this day and age there is no need to have a dog and 'suffer' with it. It really is possible to end up with a happy, fun-loving *ideal dog*. All that is necessary is to use common sense and to ensure that everyone in direct contact with the puppy applies the principles that we outline in this book correctly, and, importantly, consistently. Needless to say, this takes time and calls for real commitment. However, the rewards are innumerable. *Prevention* of possible future inappropriate behaviour, although somewhat time-consuming, is far easier and much more effective than subsequent attempts to extinguish established problems.

THE PET-OWNER BOND

Puppies and adult dogs like to be accepted members of the family. They appreciate being cuddled, caressed, played with and talked to at appropriate times. It is by actions of this sort that you can cement a strong and lasting bond between yourself and your pet. Although perhaps trite, there is much truth in the saying 'love your dog and your dog will love you and go out of his way to please'. Such a dog, one that will not even think about upsetting or disobeying his owner, is an *ideal dog*. Owners of dogs like this can be justly proud of their pet and the admiring comments he stimulates. If more pet owners achieve that goal, then our efforts in writing this book will have been well worthwhile.

CHAPTER 1

MAKING THE COMMITMENT

1. Responsibilities
2. Expenditure
3. Size
4. Coat type
5. Purpose
6. Dog or bitch?
7. Pedigree or mongrel?
8. One dog or two?

The decision to obtain a puppy implies a big commitment for you and your family. No one should even entertain the idea of rearing a puppy unless they are willing and able to take care of the pet for the next 10 years or more. It is, therefore, vital to ensure that all the family members want a dog and that a puppy is not obtained on a whim or accepted as a present.

Think into the future and make sure that you will be able to spend the time necessary to raise your puppy properly. Other responsibilities, such as full-time employment or bringing up small children, may divert too much time away from your puppy. Young puppies need lots of social contact and direction if they are to reach their full potential.

You may be tempted to see what is available and then decide whether any particular puppy takes your fancy. Invariably, however, the heart will take over and rational decisions will fly 'out of the window'. You can too easily find yourself committed to take on a pet that is entirely unsuitable for your circumstances.

Choosing a puppy is one of the most important decisions you will make in life and it cannot easily be changed or revoked. Therefore, it is most important that you consider all the pros and cons and plan accordingly.

Take time to consider all the points listed on the following pages and answer all the questions truthfully. This will help you to decide whether you are 'cut out' to be a dog owner, and, if you are, to define your preferences and draw up a profile of your *ideal dog*. Then – and only then – should you look to see what's on offer and choose the individual puppy that best meets your requirements.

1. RESPONSIBILITIES

- Do all the family members really like dogs, and will that be true for the foreseeable future? Everyone in the household will need to be involved.
- Are you particularly house- or garden-proud? Poorly behaved dogs can spoil carpets, furniture, flower beds and vegetable plots!

2. EXPENDITURE

- Can you meet the initial cost? Consider the price of a pedigree dog, the cost of vaccination, flea control and worming, and the purchase of accessories, such as crates, beds, collars, leads, toys, etc.
- Would you like to keep the initial cost low by opting for a mongrel or crossbreed? If so, note that a major drawback is that you will have much less idea of how big your pet will be when fully grown and what his coat type and inherited temperament is likely to be.
- Can your budget easily meet the ongoing maintenance costs? Big dogs cost considerably more to feed and insure, and holiday kennelling is more expensive.
- Is your property properly fenced so that your dog cannot escape and possibly cause a road traffic accident or intimidate people? Good fencing does not come cheap!

3. SIZE

Dogs come in all shapes and sizes. Miniature breeds, such as the Chihuahua, can weigh a mere 2 kgs (4 lbs). Conversely, giant breeds, such as the Great Dane, may hit the scales at more than 54 kgs (120 lbs). You should, therefore, have little trouble finding a dog to suit your preference and lifestyle.

Although the following points do not apply to *all* dogs, they are generalisations that can be used to help you decide on the size of dog you want.

- By and large, very big dogs tend to be gentle and quiet in the house, but they often have shorter lifespans than smaller dogs.

- Big dogs may be more boisterous and possibly aggressive to other dogs.
- There is plenty of choice amongst the medium-sized breeds, and most families can find their *ideal dog* from within this class.
- Small dogs may be excitable and noisy, and some terriers can be snappy, although consistent training should remove potential problems such as these. Toy breeds may be more delicate in constitution and mainly only suitable for people who lead a more sedentary life.

The current trend is towards large dogs, but the choice is yours. The percentage of the dog population in the UK in relation to size is shown in table one.

1. UK DOG OWNERSHIP (BY SIZE OF DOG)

SIZE	PERCENTAGE
Toy	7.0
Small	23.0
Medium	26.0
Large	40.5
Giant	3.5

As well as bearing in mind the above generalisations, ask yourself the following questions to determine what size of dog will suit you best.

- Do you have the time to provide adequate daily exercise? Big dogs need to be walked several miles a day!
- Is there adequate, easily accessible exercise space near at hand? Is it suitable in good and bad weather?
- Do you have enough room in your home and car for the size of dog you prefer? Will there be room for all the family and the dog when he is fully grown?
- Will you need to pick up and carry your dog or lift him into the back of a car? If so, you may like to consider a smaller breed or a dog ramp!
- Do you have, or are you expecting to have, small children in the family? Larger dogs can easily injure small children; although gentle, they can be boisterous. Small dogs can be snappy.
- Are there elderly people in the household? Old people can easily be tripped by small dogs under their feet or knocked over by larger dogs. Very small dogs are not usually suitable for large families due to their more delicate build.

2. POPULAR DOG BREEDS BY WEIGHT AND COAT TYPE

WEIGHT	COAT TYPE		
	SHORT	MEDIUM	LONG
VERY SMALL <7 kgs (<15 lbs)	Chihuahua Dachshund (Miniature Smooth-haired)	Border Terrier	Pekingese Yorkshire Terrier
SMALL 7-11 kgs (15-24 lbs)	Beagle Pug Whippet	Bichon Frisé Cavalier King Charles Spaniel Miniature Schnuzer West Highland White Terrier	Lhasa Apso Shih Tzu
MEDIUM 12-20 kgs (25-44 lbs)	Staffordshire Bull Terrier	Border Collie Cocker Spaniel English Springer Spaniel	Kerry Blue Terrier Samoyed
LARGE 21-38 kgs (45-84 lbs)	Boxer Bull Terrier Dalmatian Dobermann Labrador Retriever Weimaraner	German Shepherd Dog Golden Retriever	Afghan Hound Bearded Collie Irish Setter Rough Collie
VERY LARGE >38 kgs (>84 lbs)	Great Dane Rottweiler	Irish Wolfhound Japanese Akita	Newfoundland

- Do you have expensive ornaments that can be easily damaged by the swishing tails of large dogs? Accidents can and do happen.
- What is the attitude of your neighbours to dogs? Small dogs can be yappy. Dogs left to bark continually while owners are out are a major cause of friction.

4. COAT TYPE

You are spoilt for choice! The great variety of coat types that exist between dog breeds means that you are more likely to have difficulty deciding what you like rather than finding a breed with the coat you prefer.

You can choose a short-coated dog, such as a Dobermann or Boxer, which needs minimal grooming, or you could go for the silky coat of a spaniel, which looks great but requires daily attention. You may prefer the thick double coat of a German Shepherd or Labrador, but remember that they shed a lot of hair at certain times of the year. If the wiry coat of a terrier breed takes your fancy, remember that regular stripping or trimming is needed to keep them in shape. You can even opt for hairless dogs, or dogs that do not shed hair (e.g. Bichon Frisé or Poodle). However, first consider the points noted below.

- Have you enough spare time, patience and a suitable place in which to groom medium- and long-haired dogs daily? Long coats readily become matted if not groomed regularly. If in doubt, opt for a short-coated breed.
- Do you have sufficient time, commitment and facilities to bath your dog, albeit maybe only a few times a year but often unexpectedly? Many dogs have the unfortunate habit of deliberately rolling in unpleasant material when exercised off the lead!
- Can your funds meet the cost of paying a groomer to clip, trim or strip the dog, depending on the breed? Keeping a Poodle looking smart can be relatively costly! – unless you do it yourself.
- Are you, or anyone else in the family, allergic to dog hair? Certain breeds may be suitable, such as the Poodle, Bedlington Terrier or the Bichon Frisé, but you will need to be extremely careful where allergies are concerned.

5. PURPOSE

Some breeds evolved through selective breeding to develop their natural ability for certain tasks – herding, tracking, retrieving, guarding or companionship. Obviously it makes sense to choose a breed that has an inherent behaviour that fits most closely with what you wish to achieve.

- Do you want your dog to act as a guard dog? Some breeds will do this naturally but others will be more inclined to lick intruders to death!
- Do you want a dog to show? Bear in mind that much time and commitment is needed if you are to do this successfully, although it can be very rewarding. Whatever breed you choose, remember that you will need a top-quality specimen if you intend to show.
- Do you want to train your dog so that he can enter agility and flyball competitions? Certain breeds – Border Collies and their crosses, German Shepherds and terriers, for example – are particularly good at this.
- Do you want a dog to compete in field trials? There are plenty of dogs in the Kennel Club's Gundog group to choose from.

6. DOG OR BITCH?

Generally speaking, bitches tend to be less dominant, less pushy, and more trustworthy with children, especially those within the family. On the other hand, they do sometimes have temperament swings. Dogs, especially of the larger breeds, call for firmer handling and are, therefore, probably better suited to people who can meet this need.

DOGS
- Ask yourself if you can you afford to have your dog castrated – surgically or medically. It may be considered necessary in response to hypersexual traits that can develop in unneutered dogs, which include:
  - Roaming
  - Mounting people and inanimate objects
  - Territory marking (urinating in the home)
  - Aggression towards other dogs
  - Destructiveness
  - Overexcitability
- Is your property properly fenced so that your dog cannot escape? Some dogs can be inclined to wander, especially if a bitch in the area is 'in season'. Certain breeds, such as Beagles, have a tendency to wander more than others. Dogs that stray can be an annoyance to passers-by and are often the cause of road traffic accidents.
- Do you have the strength to control your dog (especially if he is large) should you meet a bitch in season or an aggressive dog when you are exercising him?

BITCHES
- Can you cope with a bitch when she is 'in season'? Bitches first come into season (on heat) and are attractive to male dogs from about six to 12 months of age and at six- to 12-month intervals thereafter. Close supervision and vigilance are needed at these times to prevent unwanted pregnancies. Your property will need to be securely fenced to stop your bitch from straying and to prevent the access of unwanted male visitors.
- Can you afford to pay for a bitch to be spayed? Spaying (removal of the ovaries and uterus) is advisable if you do not intend to breed from your bitch, since this operation will prevent pregnancy, false pregnancy and infection of the womb (pyometra). Furthermore, spaying will reduce the risk of mammary tumours later in life and make the bitch more consistently companionable. Most vets recommend that spaying is best carried out after the bitch has had her first season to ensure that she develops into a fit and healthy adult, physically and mentally.
- Spayed bitches can be exhibited in the show ring, but spaying may alter the coat texture of many medium- and long-haired breeds. This may put them at a disadvantage with the other competitors in their class. Spayed bitches also have a tendency to put on weight easily, which can be a disadvantage in the show ring, although careful monitoring of diet and exercise should keep this under control.
- Do you want to enter your pet in obedience competitions? 'Entire' bitches are not really suitable for this use. They need to be withdrawn when they are 'on heat' as they will distract male dogs, and their performance may be adversely affected also.
- Do your friends frequently bring their dogs to visit you? Be aware that a dog and a bitch on heat may be difficult to manage together.

7. PEDIGREE OR MONGREL?
You really have a simple choice between initial cost and predictability – you pay your money, or you take your chance! Currently it is estimated that 59 per cent of dogs in the UK are pedigree dogs.

PEDIGREE
- By choosing a pedigree puppy you gain the advantage of having a good idea of his eventual size, coat type and major behavioural traits (see table 3 on page 18).
- Is cost an issue? The initial cost of a pedigree dog is, of course, much

higher, but the 'running costs' will be equivalent to those of a mongrel of equal size.

- Are you aware that some pedigree dogs may have inherited diseases, conditions or traits that can cause problems? These may include eye disease, heart disease or skeletal defects (see Chapter Sixteen). Such risks are lower than they were, due to a conscientious effort on the part of breeders along with the Kennel Club and breed clubs. The breeder and your vet will be able to advise you of any particular hereditary problems that relate to the breed you choose.
- Do you realise that if you choose a puppy of a breed that has conventionally been docked, he may actually have a long tail? Docking is a controversial issue and you will need to seek the advice of the breeder and your veterinary surgeon on this matter.
- As a final check before buying a pedigree puppy, try to see a specimen of the breed you fancy in a friend's house and ask their opinion of the breed. If that's not possible, talk to anyone who is walking a dog of your preferred breed; most owners will be only too glad to tell you about the pros and (sometimes) the cons of that particular breed!

If you buy a pedigree dog, you should obtain from the breeder a signed and dated Breeder Registration Certificate for your puppy, together with other relevant documentation. As the new owner of the dog, you should complete the change of ownership form on the back of the Breeder Registration Certificate and return it to the Kennel Club for validation and completion. The puppy ownership will then be transferred into your name and you will receive the Kennel Club Registration Document and six-weeks' free healthcare insurance cover.

MONGRELS AND CROSSBREEDS
- Are you willing to take a gamble on your pet's eventual size, coat type and temperament? Seeing the parents before you choose your puppy will help. However, this is not always possible, especially as the sire may not be known, and, in the case of puppies from a rescue kennel, the dam might not be known either. We strongly advise that you do not obtain a puppy from a so-called 'puppy farm' or from anyone who buys in puppies simply for onward sale.
- Are you prepared to give up the time and accept the cost of having your puppy checked by a vet soon after you obtain him? It is especially important to start vaccination regimes and worming schedules in mongrel/crossbreed puppies without delay.

3. BEHAVIOUR TRAITS, EXERCISE AND GROOMING REQUIREMENTS OF THE 20 MOST POPULAR BREEDS

BREED	BEHAVIOUR						MANAGEMENT	
	Friendliness to other dogs	Trustworthiness with children	Quietness	Disinclined to wander	Disinclined to be destructive	Protective/ guarding ability	Exercise requirements	Grooming requirements
Bichon Frisé	<0>	0	0	√	√	0	*	***
Border Collie	0	<0>	<X>	<X>	<0>	√	***	**
Border Terrier	<0>	0	X	<X>	<X>	√	**	**
Boxer	<X>	<√>	0	0	<X>	√	***	*
Bull Terrier	X	<0>	0	<0>	<X>	√	**	*
Cavalier King Charles Spaniel	√	√√	0	<0>	√	<X>	**	**
Dobermann	<X>	0	<0>	<0>	<0>	√√	***	*
German Shepherd Dog	<X>	<X>	<0>	0	0	√√	***	**
Lhasa Apso	0	√	0	√	0	<0>	*	***
Miniature Schnauzer	<0>	0	X	0	0	√	**	***
Retriever (Golden)	√	√	0	0	0	0	***	**
Retriever (Labrador)	√	√	√	<0>	<0>	0	***	*
Rottweiler	<X>	<X>	0	<0>	0	√√	***	*
Shih Tzu	<0>	<0>	0	<0>	√	<0>	**	***
Spaniel (Cocker)	<0>	<X>	<X>	<0>	X	0	**	***
Spaniel (English Springer)	√	√	0	<0>	0	0	***	**
Staffordshire Bull Terrier	X	<0>	X	<0>	0	√	***	*
Weimaraner	0	<0>	0	<0>	0	<√>	***	*
West Highland White Terrier	√	√	<0>	0	0	√	**	***
Yorkshire Terrier	0	0	<X>	<0>	<0>	<0>	*	***

KEY TO TABLE 3

BEHAVIOUR TRAITS
√√   Much better than average
√   Better than average
0   Average
X   Worse than average
< >   Variable between individuals

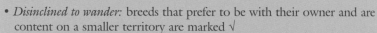

• *Disinclined to wander:* breeds that prefer to be with their owner and are content on a smaller territory are marked √
• *Disinclined to be destructive:* breeds that are less inclined than average to be destructive are marked √

Note: Many breeds of dog were bred selectively for their abilities at certain types of work, such as retrieving, guarding or herding. Many of these inherited behaviours are still present in some breeds today. For example, many terriers will be inclined to dig under fences and become escape artists; Labradors love to swim; German Shepherd Dogs may become a little too enthusiastic about guarding your home. As long as you are aware of the inherited traits your dog may show, and you are prepared for them, they should not pose too much of a problem.

EXERCISE AND GROOMING
*   Little
**   Moderate
***   Considerable

Note: Some breeds, such as the German Shepherd Dog, have double coats. These breeds need extra grooming at certain times of the year when they shed their coat. Other breeds, such as some terriers and Poodles, will need stripping and trimming – possibly professionally – if they are to stay in shape.

8. ONE DOG OR TWO?

Some prospective dog owners consider obtaining two dogs rather than just one because they believe that they will be happier together. We are of the opinion that, generally, this is not a good option for the following reasons:

• Dogs are very content to have just the attention of people as long as they are given the necessary time by their owners.
• It is not possible to give as much attention to each individual if you have more than one dog.

- It is difficult to avoid favouring one dog more than the other. This can lead to jealousy between the dogs, with constant bickering and occasionally serious fighting. The two dogs can cause major injuries to each other and the owner runs the risk of being hurt when trying to separate them. Obviously this can be a real problem with the large, powerful guarding breeds but is more easily managed in smaller breeds.
- Where there are two dogs together in one household, they will usually sort out a 'pecking order' between themselves, with you as their pack leader. However, while all may be well when you are present, in your absence things may go wrong. Our advice to novice owners is not to contemplate having two puppies from the large guarding breeds; they will need strong, experienced owners to deal with them. Many of the unfortunate serious attacks on children, other dogs, and cats have been caused by a pack of such dogs (just two is enough) running amok in the absence of the owner or not under proper control.

In our opinion, it is probably better, in most situations, to settle for just one dog, determining to give him your full, undivided attention.

If you still feel that only two dogs will do, you will have a lot of compromises to make, and great care must be taken when selecting the breeds and sex. Obviously, if you have one of either sex, unless you wish to breed, you will have to consider neutering either one or both of them. You must also consider the behaviour characteristics of the breed (see table 3 on page 18) and consider how two of your chosen breed will get along together – small breeds will probably be easier to deal with than the larger breeds.

Do not forget that you will incur more expense if you keep two dogs. If you wish to put the dogs in kennels while you go on holiday, this will prove doubly expensive, and veterinary attention and insurance will also be more costly.

CHAPTER 2

THE BREEDER

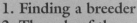

1. Finding a breeder
2. The role of the breeder
3. Golden rules of buying a puppy
4. Choosing a puppy from the litter
5. Preliminary health checks

Having decided on the breed/type of dog you would like to obtain, you will need to locate the whereabouts of a litter containing the sort of puppy you require.

1. FINDING A BREEDER
To find a reputable breeder:
- Check the advertisements in your local paper
- Contact the Kennel Club and ask for a list of breed clubs relating to your chosen breed (see Appendix 3)
- Refer to the dog press, such as *Dog World*, *Our Dogs*, *Dogs Monthly* and *Dogs Today* (see Appendix 2)
- Search the internet under breed headings (and possibly location)
- Enquire at your veterinary surgery

Having done that, and having established that the breeder has puppies of the sex you require, you will then need to go and see what's available and choose a specific puppy from within the litter.

2. THE ROLE OF THE BREEDER
It is important to make the most of the short period (three to 13 weeks of age) when puppies learn most easily and quickly

(see Chapter Six). Therefore, it is sensible to obtain a puppy from a breeder that appreciates this need.

Breeders who understand the importance of early socialisation and habituation will have raised the litter indoors, rather than in an outside kennel, or, at the very least, a mixture of both. This means that the puppy will have experienced the sounds and smells of everyday living from an early age. Such breeders will also appreciate the need to pick up the puppies regularly, so that they get used to being handled. Ideally, the breeder will have let other people see and possibly handle the young puppies. That will mean you have a head start when you come to habituate and socialise your puppy (see Chapter Six).

CANINE CARE

Breeders who have litters regularly will know that breeding bitches need to be fully vaccinated before they are mated, and wormed before whelping. They will also be aware that both the sire and the dam have been certified clinically clear of the inherited diseases that can be present in your chosen breed (see Chapter Sixteen). In most cases, good breeders will have arranged to have all the puppies in the litter given their first vaccine injection at six weeks of age.

Experienced breeders will be much more aware of the feeding requirements for small puppies. They will rear the puppies on a well-balanced, highly nutritious diet, and they will also be able to give you helpful guidance in this respect. Regular breeders usually provide the new puppy owner with a diet sheet, details of the worming routine followed, and also, where appropriate, a certificate of vaccination noting the product used and the date of administration. Registered breeders of pedigree dogs will give you a copy of the puppy's pedigree and the Kennel Club Registration Certificate and they will also advise you about the need to insure your pet.

Wherever you obtain your puppy from, check that the breeder is accustoming the puppy to household sounds and smells. If possible, arrange to have the puppy wormed, along with his first vaccination, before you take him home.

You will also need to contact your veterinary surgeon, either before you take the puppy home, or within the first few days that he is in your charge, to seek advice about vaccination, worming and feeding. This is also a good time to consider what you wish to do about insurance cover for veterinary fees should your pet fall ill during his life. The breeder or your veterinary surgeon will help you with this (see Chapter Four).

3. GOLDEN RULES OF BUYING A PUPPY

ALL PUPPIES
- Do not obtain a puppy from a 'puppy farm', where dogs are bred 'in bulk' or where litters of puppies are 'bought in' for onward sale. Similarly, do not buy a puppy from anyone who is not willing to let you see where the puppy has been reared. *Never* buy a puppy from a man in a pub, on a motorway layby, or from a service station car park!
- Take months, if necessary, to find the right litter. Do not rush into things!
- Leave children behind when viewing a litter initially.
- Never buy a puppy because you feel sorry for him.
- Never buy a sickly puppy just because he is cheaper.
- Do not buy a puppy that has been hand-reared from birth. He will not have had the chance to learn from his mother or to socialise with other puppies.
- Use your eyes. Do the bitch and the puppies appear relaxed, happy and clean? Is the bitch happy to let you see and handle her puppies? Remember that her temperament will probably be passed on to her puppies.
- Use your nose. Sickly puppies smell sour.
- It helps to obtain a puppy as soon as possible after he has reached six weeks of age. This will allow you to make full use of the early training period (see Chapter Six). However, remember that registered breeders are not allowed to sell pedigree puppies under the age of eight weeks. Furthermore, a breeder may wish to keep the puppies even longer than that, so that the ones with the best conformation can be selected for show purposes. Remember that a quality breeder should thoroughly socialise your puppy right up until the moment you are able to collect him.

PEDIGREE DOGS
- Ask if the parents have been health screened (see Chapter Sixteen) and request to see the relevant certificates.
- Ask if the breeder will provide insurance with the pup.
- Make sure that you have a signed pedigree for the pup. Ideally, you will also be given the Kennel Club registration documents when you collect your puppy. However, if they are not available at that time, get it in writing that they will be sent to you without delay.
- Get a signed receipt from the breeder, detailing any conditions under

which the puppy may be returned.
- If you are buying a bitch puppy on 'breeding terms' – where you are obliged to breed from her and let the breeder have the choice of a puppy or some puppies from the litter – make sure that the conditions are clear and unambiguous and that you are happy and able to satisfy the requirements. The breeding terms should be noted on the relevant Kennel Club form.

4. CHOOSING A PUPPY FROM THE LITTER

- Do you want an outgoing dog or a more retiring pet? The breeder will give you guidance as to which puppy is the most likely to meet your requirements in this respect. Generally, however, it makes sense to choose a puppy that is well adjusted and average in the way he reacts to people.
- Unless there are other overriding factors, do not choose a puppy that is cringing at the back of the pen, or one that appears unwell in any way. Clap your hands gently – a well-adjusted puppy should respond and allow you to pick him up without crying. The puppy should also let you hold him upright and turn him over on to his back without too much protest.
- Finally select the puppy with the colour and markings that you like.

5. PRELIMINARY HEALTH CHECKS

When choosing a puppy it is prudent to carry out a quick health check yourself. This should, of course, be backed up by a full veterinary examination after you have taken the puppy home. The vet will examine the pup to make sure that he is clear of any potential health problems that might be commonplace within the breed. The vet will also check for developmental problems that are quite frequently seen in all breeds of dogs, including mongrels and crossbreeds, such as umbilical hernias.
- **Eyes:** check that the front of the eye (the cornea) is clear and that the puppy can see with both eyes. Make sure that there is no excessive discharge from the corner of the eyes.
- **Faeces:** if possible, note the consistency of the pup's faeces. These will probably not be 'formed' as with adult dogs, but they should not be too watery, yellow or smelly. Check that the anus, and the skin around it, is not soiled or inflamed.
- **Ears:** check that the ear canals are open and that there is no discharge or odour coming from them.
- **Body:** stroke the puppy all over to ensure that there are no wounds,

swellings, abrasions or hair loss in any area. Check closely if the puppy shows any signs of pain when you touch him on his skin and gently squeeze his chest or abdomen. Check that the umbilicus (belly button) is normal and not inflamed or excessively protruding; this could indicate the presence of an umbilical hernia, which, although not necessarily serious, may necessitate surgical correction later in life.

- **Jaw:** check that the upper and lower jaw meet properly. Some breed standards call for jaws that are undershot, but generally the teeth should meet in a scissor bite – the top teeth closely overlapping the bottom teeth.
- **Feeding:** try to watch the puppy feeding to satisfy yourself that he can swallow normally.
- **Dew claws and tail:** if the puppy has had his dew claws removed or his tail docked, check that the wounds have healed normally and are not inflamed or sore.
- **Genital organs:** check that these look normal and are not red and/or swollen. Male puppies should have two normally descended testicles by two to three months of age but sometimes they descend later than this. If you are concerned, seek a veterinary opinion. Retained testicles have health implications.

If you identify anything that causes you concern, either seek further advice or consider looking for another puppy.

CHAPTER 3

PREPARING FOR YOUR PUPPY

1. Setting house rules
2. Equipment
3. The first night

Before bringing your puppy home, it pays to make all the necessary preparations beforehand. This will save you a lot of trouble in the long-run and will help to avoid many potential problems.

1. SETTING HOUSE RULES

Dogs like to know where they stand – what is permissible, what is out of bounds, and what is acceptable behaviour. To achieve this calls for a lot of careful pre-thought. The house rules you choose must be accepted and agreed by *all* members of the family. It is important that they are applied consistently and fairly by everyone, as any mistakes can take a lot of undoing.

House rules are, of course, a matter of individual choice but the following suggestions are recommended.

- Bedrooms should be out of bounds. Possibly, all upstairs rooms and and the landing should be included in this. The landing is a commanding place to lie, so it is certainly best out of bounds for pushy big dogs.
- Ideally, dogs should not allowed on the furniture, and certainly not uninvited.
- Make sure your dog has his own bed. If the dog has somewhere of his own to lie quietly and undisturbed, he is far less likely to try

muscling in on human furniture!
- Dining rooms must be out of bounds when people are eating.
- People have preference over dogs. People must be allowed to go through doorways before the dog, to eat before the dog, etc. Dogs that are lying in a doorway must be made to move; don't step over them.
- Games must be initiated and ended by people, and must not involve teasing.
- Dogs must eat food out of their own bowl only, either in the kitchen or another place you have designated for meals. Never give your dog food from your own plate or feed him tidbits while you are eating. This will encourage begging behaviour, and while it may be 'cute' in a young puppy, it can be extremely annoying in an adult dog. Start as you mean to go on.
- With the exception of dry food, a dog's meal should be picked up if it has not been eaten within 15-20 minutes.
- It is okay to lift a puppy or a small dog on to your lap and to pet, cuddle or stroke him, but this must take place at your instigation. Do not respond if your dog seeks such attention, tempting though it might be. It is much better to give him a simple command and then reward the dog with much fuss and attention if he responds correctly.
- Small, tight spaces under furniture and beds should be made 'out of bounds' because it may be difficult to get the dog out from such a 'den' later in life if he becomes frightened or aggressive for some reason.
- Human clothes and shoes are not for chewing. Provide your puppy with some acceptable chews and toys of his own. Hard rubber chews, 'raggers' (washable, plaited rope toys) or other proprietary toys are ideal. Old shoes or other household items should not be used. Your dog will not be able to tell the difference between old and new, and you will only have yourself to blame if he then eats your best shoes! If your puppy does misbehave in this way, do not throw a tantrum, just take the item away and resolve to remove any similar objects out of harm's way. Think 'prevention' and regard misdeeds as your fault!
- Do not let your dog do anything as a puppy that you will not want him to do as an adult!

In the context of house rules, remember that prevention is better than cure. If anyone sees your puppy about to commit a 'sin', they should distract him. Teach your puppy the meaning of the word **"No"** (said sharply in a disapproving tone, but not shouted) accompanied by a disapproving gesture. Follow with a command for a simple learnt response like **"Sit"** (see Chapter Nine), which can then be rewarded.

There is no harm in following the word **"No"** with a sentence or two explaining why. For example, "No! I don't want you to do that!" or "No! Chairs are for people not dogs!" Although the dog will not understand the words, he is intelligent enough to pick up your meaning and your displeasure from the tone of your voice. This all helps to reinforce the fact that a 'sin' has been committed. In sensitive dogs your disapproving attitude alone can be an effective chastisement or deterrent.

Finally, there are two small cautionary notes you must bear in mind:

- Firstly, make sure that no one in the family cheats and tries to gain favour with the dog by giving too much praise, attention and too may tidbits.
- Secondly, there can be a temptation to spoil your dog by making him altogether too dependant on you. Do not make the mistake of treating your dog as a child substitute.

2. EQUIPMENT

Having chosen your puppy, established the house rules, and worked out what, when and where your dog is allowed to go, you need to obtain all the equipment that a puppy needs.

BOWLS

Obtain good-quality drinking and feeding bowls for your dog's unique use. Choose bowls that can be cleaned easily and that sit firmly on the ground so that the contents are not readily spilt if knocked. Ceramic bowls have the advantage of weight, but stainless steel are non-breakable. Plastic bowls work perfectly well but they are not recommended generally because most puppies cannot resist chewing them!

COLLARS

When you first get your puppy, buy a small, soft collar and put it on for very short periods. Always make sure you are around when the puppy has his collar on. The first time you put the collar around the puppy's neck, try playing a game to distract his attention away from the collar. If he looks agitated after a little while, take off the collar before he starts getting really worried and scratching continually at it. Repeat the exercise later and give praise for longer periods of tolerance. Over time, your puppy will become used to wearing a collar.

As your puppy grows, buy progressively bigger collars (you may need to buy several before your puppy becomes fully mature). The collar should fit comfortably – it should not be too tight, but neither should it be so loose that it can become lost or caught up on protruding objects. Some types of collars suit certain breeds best, and your breeder should be able to advise you about this. Be wary of buying a so-called 'choke chain'. While these can look good on bigger, short-coated breeds, like Dobermanns for example, their use is highly controversial. Many trainers consider them to be at best unnecessary and at worst cruel. Misuse can cause serious injury. You should also remember that choke chains are not a substitute for taking the time to train your puppy to walk on a lead correctly.

Head or face collars are especially useful for dogs that tend to pull on the lead, or those that lunge at other dogs. This is because the control point is under the chin rather than round the neck. Control walking harnesses are useful for dogs that have any neck injuries, as they take pressure away from the neck region. They have also been used with success with larger breeds that do not take well to head collars, since they discourage pulling on the lead by exerting pressure under the arm pits. Old fashioned harnesses are rather outdated and have no place with big, strong dogs, since the owner has virtually no control. Furthermore they can interfere with the dog's natural gait.

LEADS
As with a collar, do not be tempted to economise when it comes to buying a lead; money spent on a good-quality leather or webbing lead with a robust hook/clip for attaching to the 'D' ring in the collar will be a good investment. An extendible lead, which has up to 30 ft (9 m) of lead, is also a good buy. It can also be a very useful aid when teaching a dog the recall (i.e. to come when called). If you have a large breed, however, check the strength of the line.

BED AND BEDDING
All dogs need a bed of adequate size placed in the corner of one room in the home – usually the kitchen. From the very beginning, train your puppy using the methods described in Chapter Nine, to go to his bed by saying "Go to your basket!" or "In your box!" or whatever phrase you choose, accompanied by a gesture pointing to where the bed is kept. Never forget to reward the puppy with praise and a tidbit when he responds correctly. However, be wary that you do not make going to bed a form of punishment.

Beds come in a variety of materials and those sold through reputable pet shops are all suitable. However, be aware that the most comfortable, padded, fleece-lined beds are perfect for a puppy's tiny teeth to chew on when bored! You might want to purchase a practical hard plastic oval bed that will stand up to the persistent chewing of puppy teeth. These beds are also the most hygienic. Alternatively, you can use a cardboard box with an entrance cut out of it. These are cheap and easy to replace when they have been chewed. Once your puppy has grown out of the chewing phase, you can then purchase a longer-lasting bed.

Old blankets, specially manufactured dog blankets made of polyester fleece, and bean bags with detachable covers that can be washed are all ideal as bedding. Give these a good shake, air daily, and wash frequently to keep them fresh and free from odour. If you have any doubts about beds and bedding, the breeder, pet shop manager or staff at your veterinary surgery will be prepared to give you advice on the equipment most suitable for your dog.

GROOMING TOOLS
Obtain a good-quality comb, preferably with rounded teeth, with the teeth inset into the back (spine). You will also need a brush suitable for your dog's coat. As coat care can vary significantly according to breed, you might like to seek the advice of your puppy's breeder or your vet.

TOYS
There is a huge variety of 'doggy' toys. Select just two or three of the right size for your dog and make sure that they will resist chewing and rough play. Be sure to include a good ball that is neither too hard nor too soft. Make sure that any toy you select does not have hard or sharp edges or is of such a size that it could be swallowed whole and become stuck in your dog's throat. This is particularly important in respect to balls. Do not give children's toys to your puppy – there is a strong possibility that your dog will be able to pull parts from the toy and choke. Also be wary of soft/squeaky toys, as puppies are easily able to pull these apart and ingest the stuffing or 'squeak', possibly with dire consequences.

DOG CRATES/PLAY-PENS
Collapsible wire crates, which are also known as indoor kennels or play-pens, are an extremely useful addition to a house with a new puppy. Crates are easily erected in the house (usually in the kitchen), garden or the back of a car. The crate needs to be large enough to accommodate your dog comfortably when he is fully grown, although you could buy a small crate to begin with and then a larger larger one as your pup matures. There needs to be adequate room for him to stand up and lie down stretched out.

Crates provide a safe haven for your puppy if you have to leave him unsupervised for a short time. Furthermore, it will help to prevent the puppy from doing any wrong that will subsequently call for corrective procedures. However, never keep your puppy in his crate for extended periods of time, and never use the crate as a form of punishment.

• Crates are made of wire panels that fold down into the size of a suitcase for carrying. Most models have a metal tray floor. They are quick to erect.

• A crate helps with housetraining – the door can be shut when the pup is asleep and opened when he wakes up and is taken outside to relieve himself.

• As they are portable, crates can be taken into any room in the house, placed in the garden, or fixed in the back of an estate car. However, remember that, even in a crate, a dog should not be left in a car for lengthy periods and never if it is sunny. Don't forget that dogs cannot rid themselves of body heat in the same way as humans, and, with the car windows magnifying the strength of the sun's rays, even on a fairly cool day the inside of a car can become a death trap for a dog.

• Crates are ideal if you go visiting friends who are not keen on dogs. They can also be used when your dog is ill and needs protection, rest and nursing.

• Crates can be obtained from most pet shops or pet superstores, where you can also obtain further advice about their use.

• Play-pens are essentially large crates. They form a safe retreat where dogs can see and be seen, in much the same way as a children's play-pen is used. They act as a den – a place that offers your dog protection.

FIGURE 4.

Dog crates are ideal for confining your puppy for short periods while you are out, overnight, or to help with housetraining.

Play-pens are particularly useful to dog breeders because they can be used to accommodate a bed for a bitch and her puppies, a space to place feeding and drinking bowls, and room for the pups to move about when they first find their feet. This provides safety for the bitch and pups, and allows breeders to keep an eye on them at all times.

3. THE FIRST NIGHT

Before you bring home your puppy, think about how you are going to handle his first night at home. Get it right and you will have 'cracked it' forever, but get it wrong and it could take you months to undo. Remember that, while you may be highly excited about your new arrival, your puppy will be feeling bewildered by the whole experience and will be missing his mother and littermates.

Opinion is divided on whether it is better to let your puppy spend his first night in your bedroom or downstairs snug in his own bed. We feel that the latter option is best, particularly if you are trying to establish your position as 'pack leader' and have therefore made bedrooms 'out of bounds'. This stipulation is much easier to enforce if it has never been breached. If you don't intend that your dog will sleep in your bedroom as an adult, don't let him do so as a puppy! Furthermore, you will have to move your pup's sleeping area from your bedroom to a downstairs room at some point. It makes far more sense to go through a period of disturbed sleep just once, rather than once again when you move your pup. By that time, your puppy will be older and bigger and quite capable of making a lot of noise and fuss, scratching at the doors. He will be much more likely to become anxious and fearful.

We recommend that, during the first afternoon and evening, you entertain your new puppy so that he is pleasantly tired. Feed his last meal around 6pm, not forgetting to take him out to relieve himself immediately afterwards. Just before you retire to bed, take your puppy outside again, stay with him (regardless of the weather) and encourage him to 'perform'. When he 'goes' give him lavish praise and a small tidbit (see Chapter Eight for more information on housetraining).

When you come back inside, place your pup in his crate or basket, in the kitchen, with a warm hot-water bottle or reheatable warming pad wrapped in a blanket. The crate or play-pen should not be too large, although it must be big enough to allow the puppy to stand up, turn around and lie down comfortably. Most dogs are reluctant to go to the toilet near eating or sleeping areas, and this is why crates are invaluable during housetraining.

TAKING ON A PUPPY

Puppies are irresistible, but you need to think long and hard before taking on the commitment of owning a dog.

CHOOSING A BREED

The Border Collie loves to work, and needs plenty of mental stimulation.

You will need to have the house space – and car space – for a breed as big as the Pyrenean Mountain Dog.

The Labrador Retriever is an excellent family dog, and remains one of the most popular of all breeds.

Like many of the Toy breeds, the Pomeranian is small in stature but big on personality.

The Parson Jack Russell Terrier is a feisty, spirited dog who thrives on an active lifestyle.

The spectacular-looking Dalmatian is built on athletic lines and needs lots of exercise.

CHOOSING A BREED

The Beagle is a handy size and will adapt to town or country living.

A crossbreed is the product of parents of two known breeds, such as this Labrador/ Golden Retriever cross.

A mongrel is the product of two non-pedigree dogs, and can be any size, shape or temperament!

GROOMING REQUIREMENTS

You will need to enjoy grooming if you take on a long-coated breed, such as the Bearded Collie.

Many of the terrier breeds, like this West Highland White Terrier, need to have their coats stripped on a regular basis.

It takes a tremendous amount of work to keep the glamorous Yorkshire Terrier in full coat.

VIEWING THE LITTER

You should see the mother with her puppies when you visit the breeder.

The puppies should be clean and healthy, and appear interested in everything that is going on.

Watch the puppies play together and you will see their individual personalities begin to emerge.

CARING FOR YOUR PUPPY

Your pup will soon learn to settle in his crate.

Stick to the diet that the breeder recommends – at least to begin with.

It is a legal requirement for your dog to have some form of visible identification.

From the moment you take your new puppy home, you are responsible for all his needs.

Ensure that the bedding covers the whole floor area of the crate. Underneath the bedding provide a thick pad of newspaper that can be discarded if it becomes wet or soiled. It is also useful to include a small piece of bedding given to you by the breeder, as it will have the smell of the puppy's mother and littermates on it. You can, if you like, leave a ticking clock nearby in the room to serve as a cue to the puppy that you will return or maybe just to take the place of his mother's heart beat.

Speak soothingly to the puppy, give him a farewell pat and another small tidbit and then retire. It is crucial that you follow the same routine every night. Leave a light on in the hall to provide a low light from under the door, and draw any blinds or curtains. Go upstairs quietly and without any fuss, and, with luck, your puppy should fall asleep promptly. If he doesn't, or if he wakes later in the night and cries, come down quickly and check he is okay. Do not scold him, just pick him up and take him outside to be clean. Do nothing that the pup can construe as a reward for crying. When he has 'performed' outside, praise and 'jolly' him and go through the whole routine again.

The first night you must be prepared to go through the routine two or even three times. The next night may require just two visits. By the third night, you will be disturbed just the once – if at all – hopefully! Be prepared, needless to say, to wake by 6 or 7am for the first week – to give your pup a 'fair chance'.

Never scold your pup if he has had an accident during the night. Just clean up. However, if your puppy has been good and clean, go overboard in your praise. With luck, your pup will learn to go through the night from 11pm to 7am within just seven to eight days.

This training method is not in any way cruel and serves the purpose of emphasising that you are the leader and that you cannot be manipulated easily. By following it, you will achieve your goal more quickly and will soon end up with a happy, cheerful *ideal dog* that is quite content to be left on his own at night.

CHAPTER 4

THINKING AHEAD

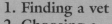

As with many things in life, the key to successful dog ownership is preparation. No matter how much love and attention you lavish on your dog, things can come crashing down around you if you have failed to think about the future and what you would do in certain situations. As an example, think about what would happen if your dog becomes suddenly violently ill during the night. If you have already registered your puppy with a vet, you can seek help immediately. Otherwise, you may end up wasting valuable time while you trawl through the local telephone directory, and even then you would not be assured that the vet you have chosen on the spur of the moment is the best vet for you and your particular dog. Think too about what would happen if your puppy were to escape. If you haven't taken steps to ensure that your dog has identification on him at all times, can you be absolutely sure that you and he will be happily reunited? If you prepare for as many eventualities as possible, you will save yourself a lot of time, money and heartache in the long run.

1. FINDING A VET

Once you have your puppy at home you should, without delay, set about finding a veterinary practice with which you are comfortable and which can

supply the services you are likely to require. You will need to find a vet you can relate to and who will take a genuine interest in your dog.

When it comes to choosing a vet, there is much more involved than simply choosing the one closest to your home. Personal recommendation is, by far, the best route. Ask the advice of your breeder, and also ask friends and acquaintances who have dogs. There is a wide choice of veterinary practices in most areas and it is certainly sensible to visit a number before making your choice; this will allow you to see for yourself what is on offer. It is far better to make a reasoned choice in advance than to wait until you need help at short notice in an emergency.

The Royal College of Veterinary Surgeons offers a 'find a vet' service via the internet. If you need help, visit www.findavet.org.uk.

Also consider the points noted below to help ensure that you get it right.

- **Location:** proximity of the surgery to your home and ease of parking. These factors are undoubtedly important but should not be an overriding consideration.
- **Specialisation:** does the practice concentrate on the treatment of pets or does it offer a wider service to horse owners and farmers? In the latter case, will the larger animals take preference in an emergency?
- **Consultations:** are these by appointment or is there an open surgery? Which would you prefer? Do the surgery hours fit in with your time commitments? Is the surgery open at weekends and over Christmas and other public holidays? What is the average consultation fee?
- **House visits:** does the vet make house calls out of hours in an emergency, or is it practice policy to do consultations only at the surgery? Do you have suitable transport available at all hours?
- **Size of practice:** practices that employ several vets can obviously offer fuller cover. They are also more likely to have better and more modern equipment, and kennelling space should there be the need to keep an animal overnight. Often, in large practices, some vets will specialise in a particular area of veterinary medicine or surgery, minimising the need for pets to be referred for a second opinion with a consultant somewhere else in the country. However, a drawback with large, multi-vet practices is that you might not always see the same person each time you visit, even for an ongoing problem. Furthermore, the service is likely to be somewhat less personal.
- **Premises:** it is not unreasonable to ask, pleasantly, if it would be possible for you to be shown around the premises. This will allow you to assess the practice's attitude towards cleanliness, tidiness and the general equipment and facilities it has to offer. In most cases, you will

doubtless be impressed; in which case don't forget to give praise where praise is due.

- **Practice nurses:** does the practice employ trained lay staff? Qualified veterinary nurses can be a very helpful source of information and they often run special clinics, at reasonable prices, for puppies and overweight dogs, etc.
- **Charges:** be prepared to ask about standard charges for consultations, vaccinations and routine operations.
- **Veterinary hospitals:** some practices have hospital status granted by the Royal College of Veterinary Surgeons, which goes a long way to guaranteeing the service given and the range that can be offered. Overnight accommodation with nursing attendance is also available in these establishments.

2. CHOOSING A BOARDING KENNEL

It is quite possible that you will need to board your dog while you are on holiday or if you are faced with some emergency. It makes a lot of sense, therefore, to spend time choosing a boarding kennel in advance rather than making a hurried selection at a time of need.

First, discuss the matter with your friends, with other dog owners and with the staff at your veterinary surgery. Personal recommendation counts for a lot. Secondly, visit a number of local kennels to check and compare premises. Ask yourself the following questions:

- Do the premises appear clean and well run?
- Are the buildings in good condition and secure?
- Can you relate to the owner and the staff?
- Look at the dogs in the kennel. Are they in good condition, are they clean, and do they appear happy and well fed?
- Are the dogs housed separately, and is there an individual run attached to each kennel?
- What other exercise facilities are there?
- What is the owner's policy about preventive vaccination? A good kennel will insist on dogs having up-to-date vaccinations.
- Does the boarding establishment offer an insurance scheme to cover emergency care should your dog fall ill while you are away?

If the answers to all these questions are satisfactory, ask if you could board your puppy for a night or two, on a couple of separate occasions, when he is five to six months old. This serves two purposes. Firstly, it allows you to check that your dog can be left safe and happy away from you, but with you available in case all is not well. Secondly, it will familiarise your puppy with the boarding kennel. His short kennelling experience will imprint on his mind that boarding is only a temporary thing, and not for life!

Whenever you leave your dog in kennels, make sure that the owner knows how to contact you while you are away, in case an emergency should arise. If you need to board your dog, make a note to book him into the kennel of your choice as far in advance as possible; good kennels can become fully booked very quickly.

Finally, be very wary of leaving your dog at home in the charge of a neighbour or friend when you go on holiday. It is a big responsibility that is much better left to professionals. However, if a boarding kennel is not an option for whatever reason, you may find it useful to contact the National Association of Pet Sitters (see Appendix Two).

3. SAFETY

Like people, dogs can have serious accidents all too easily. If you follow the tips noted below, these risks will be kept to a minimum. The diligent dog owner will always be aware of, and alert to, possible dangers, and they will take steps to ensure their dog's safety. Think ahead and look out for possible dangers. Table 5 on pages 46 and 47 will, hopefully, give you some guidance.

4. YOUR DOG AND THE LAW

Although it is no longer a legal requirement to have a licence if you own a dog, there remain a number of criteria that, by law, you must comply with as a dog owner.

- You must ensure that your dog is not a nuisance to other people. This includes persistent barking, trespassing on other people's property, threatening or attacking people, and obstructing access to a public place or roadway.
- It is an offence to abandon a dog, including leaving him at home, without regular attention and the provision of food and water.
- Your dog must wear some form of identification (see below).
- It is an offence to let your dog worry livestock. You could be prosecuted and your dog could be destroyed for such an offence.
- It is an offence to allow a dog to travel in a vehicle in a way that will cause suffering.
- It is an offence to make a dog pull a wheeled vehicle on a public highway.

5. KEEP YOUR

INDOORS

Protect open fires with a fire guard.

Ensure that electrical leads are out of reach and that all electrical appliances are properly earthed and are connected to a fused plug.

Keep all cleaning products, including detergents and disinfectants, out of reach and preferably in high-up cupboards.

Discard rubber bands properly and promptly. They can only too easily become fixed around a dog's tongue, paw or tail with disastrous consequences.

Dogs are better kept out of bathrooms and kitchens. When cooking, hot liquids can easily be spilt.

Keep rubbish bins firmly shut.

Make sure that all large and valuable ornaments are out of reach and placed securely so that they will not fall.

Some house plants can be poisonous or irritating to dogs and should be kept out of reach. If in doubt, consult a good houseplant manual or check at a garden centre.

Never give dogs chocolate as a treat. Even small quantities can cause illness or possibly death. Dark chocolate is especially dangerous. Dog owners should use garden composts that do not contain cocoa shell mulch and should keep all products containing chocolate securely shut away. Choc drops especially formulated for dogs are quite safe.

Make sure that dog toys are not too hard, nor too soft and that they don't have sharp edges or are small enough to be swallowed whole. They should withstand chewing and rough play, and be discarded when they are worn out.

Give specially merchandised dog chews rather than bones of any description.

Never leave your dog loose and unattended with babies or young children no matter how well mannered he is – even for a moment.

DOG SAFE

OUTDOORS

Ensure that food put out for birds and wild animals cannot be reached by your dog. Pick up any dead birds or animals.

Keep hedgerows clear.

Avoid growing mistletoe, yew trees and laburnum and a number of other plants that can be poisonous to your dog. Seek advice from a good garden centre.

Take particular care if dogs have access to a garage or garden shed. Antifreeze, old paint, wood preservatives, glues, weed killers, fungicides and slug pellets are all of particular concern. Consequently, garages and sheds are best kept firmly shut and declared 'out of bounds'.

Use garden sprays very carefully and don't allow your dog access to sprayed areas at least until the spray is dry on the leaves.

Remove drinking bowls before spraying with weed killer or dusting with ant powder, etc.

Make sure that swimming pools and ponds are dog safe.

Keep your dog on the lead on busy roads no matter how obedient he is, and put him on a lead before you get out of the car with him.

Check garden boundaries regularly.

Make sure all rubbish from the house or garden is securely wrapped and placed in a dustbin that can be properly closed.

Travelling with a dog loose in a car is not illegal as long as the dog does not interfere with the driver. However, it is sensible to fit a dog guard, use a dog crate firmly fixed to the back seat, or restrain your dog in a purpose-designed dog harness. A 30mph crash would throw a 50lb dog forward with enough force to injure him severely and to possibly kill the driver or a passenger! Small dogs can travel safely in the foot well in front of the passenger, at least for short distances, but they do prefer to see where they are going! Do not let your dog put his head outside through a car window.

- It is an offence to cause suffering to a dog, in any way, by neglect or deliberate cruelty.
- The Veterinary Surgeons Act 1966 (Section 19) states that, subject to a number of exceptions, only registered members of the Royal College of Veterinary Surgeons may practise veterinary surgery. 'Veterinary surgery' is defined within the Act as encompassing the 'art and science of veterinary surgery and medicine', which includes the diagnosis and surgical operations that may not necessarily form part of a treatment. These restrictions are in the interests of ensuring that animals are treated only by people qualified to do so. Details relating to the exceptions can be obtained from the Internet by visiting www.rcvs.org.uk. Two particular exceptions are of relevance to the new puppy owner:
  1. Anyone administering emergency first aid to an animal to save life, or to relieve pain or suffering.
  2. Behavioural treatment modification methods that do not involve an act of veterinary surgery.
- It is an offence to allow your dog to be dangerously out of control in a public place.
- By law, car drivers who hit a dog must report the incident to the police at the earliest opportunity.
- Local by-laws ban fouling by dogs in fixed areas. Owners can be fined if they do not pick up faeces passed by their dog in these places. All responsible dog owners should pick up their dog's faeces as a matter of course.

5. IDENTIFICATION

Dog owners are legally required to ensure that their dog wears a collar and tag at all times when the dog is away from their own property. There are a number of alternative means of identification that are now available, which – in the case of tattoos or micro-chipping – have the added advantage of being permanent. This means that, should your dog lose his collar at the same time he goes missing, he can still be readily identified, and, hopefully, returned to you safe and well.

DOG TAGS

It is mandatory for all dogs to wear a tag (usually an engraved metal disc) attached to their collars. This should show the owner's name, address, telephone number, and, possibly, the dog's name. Owners are responsible for ensuring that the lettering on the tag does not become blurred, that it can be easily read, and that the information is up to date. It is a good idea to include the name and telephone number of your dog's vet on the tag as well, in case of emergencies.

TATTOOS

Tattooing is a proven permanent method of identification that is recognised by the Companion Animal Welfare Council (CAWC). The dog is marked, using indelible ink, with a seven-figure number on either the ear flap, or, less commonly, the inside of the thigh. Puppies can be tattooed before they are homed, usually when they are six to eight weeks of age. The procedure is relatively quick, but the services of a skilled tattooist are needed, which can be expensive. The tattoo mark is recorded by a central body that may be contacted if a stray is found to establish the dog's identity and to locate the owner.

There are two main disadvantages of tattooing. It is not an acceptable method of identification for the Pet Travel Scheme (PETS), and, the ink may fade over time, which may necessitate further tattooing. However, tattooing does have the advantage of being a quick and visible method of identification that can discourage theft.

When exporting dogs to some countries, such as Canada, a tattoo is a necessary requirement.

MICRO-CHIPS

The 'state-of-the-art' identity marker is undoubtedly the implanted identity 'chip'. This is a small, bar-coded pellet that is implanted between the shoulder blades at the base of the dog's neck. The implant can be put in place when puppies are just a few weeks old. The chip lasts for life, cannot be altered, and can easily be 'read' by a transponder, like the instrument used to read barcodes in supermarket checkouts. Most major rescue homes have these 'readers', as do the police, local authorities and the majority of veterinary surgeries. Information relating to the dog and its owner can be obtained from a central database when the number encoded on the chip has been identified.

Chipping is not difficult, and can, in fact, be carried out by any trained person; veterinary qualification is not required. Properly done, the procedure is painless for the dog – the actual chip being no larger than a grain of rice. Ideally, the microchip should be checked regularly every time the dog is taken to a veterinary surgery, to ensure that it is still working and that it has not moved to another site (such as the shoulder or the elbow). The more modern micro-chips have a special device that helps prevent 'migration' from the site of implantation.

Micro-chipping has become the most popular method of permanently identifying dogs. It is recognised by the British Small Animal Veterinary Association as being safe and reliable. The Kennel Club runs 'Petlog'; (see Appendix Two), which is the largest pet identification and reunification scheme in the UK for dogs that have been micro-chipped.

To qualify for the Pet Travel Scheme (PETS) dogs must be implanted with a microchip so that they can be properly identified. Full details about regulations, governing the taking of dogs overseas and for dogs entering or re-entering the UK, can be obtained from PETS/DEFRA (see Appendix Two).

6. INSURANCE

All dog owners should have public liability insurance, which will indemnify them in the case of accidents to the general public or damage to their property. It is indeed possible that third-party insurance will become a legal requirement for dog owners in the UK in the future. Household insurance policies sometimes provide cover for the owner, but not the dog. Therefore, your dog will be covered only when he is in the care and control of you, the insured householder, or your family.

Dog owners can, if they wish, cover the cost of veterinary attention, in the case of accident or illness. Although insurance premiums have increased lately, the cover provided is still good value. The cost of veterinary treatment has risen dramatically in recent years, as diagnostic aids have become more complex and are employed more often. Furthermore, drugs and equipment are much more expensive these days, and the referral of difficult cases to a specialist vet is more frequently recommended.

Generally, standard insurance policies cover:
- Veterinary fees, often including complementary medicine.
- Early death from illness or accident; reimbursement of the purchase price of the dog.
- Third-party liability and legal expenses.
- Costs involved in recovering a lost dog.
- Loss by theft or straying; reimbursement of purchase price.
- Emergency boarding kennel fees.
- Holiday cancellation costs.
- Veterinary attention during overseas travel.

Insurance policies do not normally cover:
- Preventative vaccination.

- Elective neutering.
- Caesarean section.
- Death of a bitch peri-natally.
- Death of newborn puppies.

Pet insurance is offered by a number of insurance companies, organisations and associations. The policies available vary quite considerably in detail; a variety of discounts are given and differing excesses applied. The cost is also affected by such considerations as where you live, the size and breed of your dog, and a number of other factors. As a result, it can be difficult to compare like with like. If you are in doubt, seek the advice of your veterinary surgeon. Most will have first-hand experience of what is available and many (those who are authorised to do so) can give you guidance as to the best buy for your circumstances.

If you are considering breeding from your bitch, it makes sense to check with the insurer to establish whether any of the risks associated with whelping are covered, and, if not, to establish the likely cost of doing so.

Some policies, such as the Kennel Club's Healthcare Plan, offer additional benefits, such as a veterinary helpline, bereavement counselling, legal advice and a pet minder helpline. At least one company covers the cost of using special diets for life.

CHAPTER 5

CANINE COMMUNICATION

1. The language of dogs
2. Reading the signs

In the past, many biologists have talked about the importance of recognising the differences between species. Recently, however, more scientists have reached the conclusion that species have much more in common physiologically than they have differences. For example, all animals have a digestive tract, a respiratory tract, a circulatory system and a nervous system. These all 'work' in a similar way, regardless of species. All animals have these systems regulated by hormones and controlled by enzymes.

That said, it is true that some relatively small differences have been developed by some species to enable them to adapt to the environment in which they find themselves. Cows, for example, have four stomachs to help them digest vegetable matter more efficiently. The teeth of carnivores have become adapted for tearing and cutting flesh. Camels have a hump, horses have hooves, moles are designed for burrowing, and so on.

1. THE LANGUAGE OF DOGS

Dogs and people follow this pattern of similarity except for a major difference – people have developed the power of speech. Dogs, on the other hand, can neither talk nor truly understand the spoken word. In behavioural terms, this means that dogs cannot be taught, as we can, by being told of other people's experiences. Furthermore, they cannot ask the important questions of What? When? Why? How? Think how much more quickly a dog would learn if he could ask "Have I responded as you want?" "Why are you cross with me?" and "What have I done wrong?"

Although dogs are not able to talk, they communicate using their own sophisticated method – body language. As a result, and because they don't have any distractions – reading books, watching television, and spending time on the internet – dogs have become very astute observers. They can, without doubt, detect minute changes in the attitude of humans. Dog owners often remark "My dog can always tell when it's bedtime" or "My dog knows that we will be going on holiday tomorrow". Dogs often seem to know when they are about to be left in kennels, possibly by picking up the sense of anticipation and excitement in their owners with the prospect of a holiday in mind.

We humans have also developed the ability to detect what other people mean by observing small changes in facial expression, the shrug of the shoulders and even minute changes in iris size (sometimes we have difficulty 'reading' people who wear dark glasses). We also know when people don't really mean what they are saying! This innate and learnt ability is particularly noticeable when driving a car. Think about how easily you are often able to tell, from a distance, whether or not a passer-by is looking at you or so engrossed in their own thoughts that they are oblivious. But dogs go far, far beyond this ability. Indeed, it often seems that they are aware of our thoughts before we actually do anything.

From a behavioural point of view, we can learn to 'understand' our dogs to a much greater degree if we learn to read and interpret their body language. We will also get more response from our dogs if we use our adaptation of their body language, together with words, when we teach them how to behave. The value of using gestures and words is often underestimated, and it is certainly far more effective than shouting!

Learning the language of dogs has many more consequences than simply making our dogs understand what we want them to do, however. Often, and quite unintentionally, we encourage or 'reinforce' a dog's behaviour by an inadvertent gesture that the dog reads as praise or admonishment. It is a fact that many inappropriate behaviours in dogs stem from this cause. Often, all that is needed is to analyse precisely what the owner is doing and how the dog could interpret it, and then to stop the action or gesture and never repeat it. The unwanted behaviour will then, frequently and quite promptly, 'extinguish' itself.

2. READING THE SIGNS

A dog's emotions and intentions can be read by observing his stance, how he holds his ears and tail, and his facial expression. It pays to observe your pet closely as a puppy, and throughout his life, so that you can interpret what he is 'saying' to you. Some of the more common signs are noted here.

For completeness, it should be noted that, besides using body language to communicate, dogs also make sounds (vocalisation). A rumbling growl is used as a warning, but a low throat murmur is used as a sign of pleasure by some dogs when they are petted. Howling, always done from the standing position, is used as a distress call and for dog-to-dog communication. The sound can carry a very long way and is never used in conjunction with aggression.

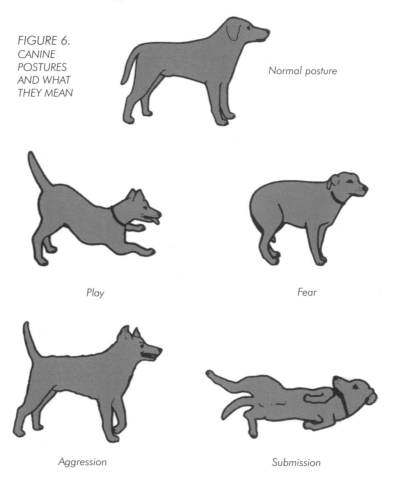

FIGURE 6. CANINE POSTURES AND WHAT THEY MEAN

Normal posture

Play

Fear

Aggression

Submission

7. CANINE BODY LANGUAGE		
SIGN/POSTURE		**INTERPRETATION**
EARS	Pricked/erect pointing forward	Dog alert and listening – "I'm interested, what do you want?"
	Held back to head	Submission, pleasure or ready to attack – "Take care!"
	Flat back or low on head	Fear – "I'm sorry, don't punish me!"
EYES	Narrowed and half closed	Pleasure or submission – "You may approach!"
	Wide open and staring	Threatening – "I'm the boss, don't challenge me!"
	Soft-eyed, sideways glance	Approval – "I like your style!"
MOUTH	One-sided grin	A friendly greeting – "You can come closer!"
	Both lips pulled back to expose teeth	The start of aggression – "Look out!"
	Head lowered, not barking	"I'm about to mount an imminent attack – advance at your peril!"
BODY	Standing on toes, chest thrust forward, erect hair on neck and along back	Aggression – "I mean business"
	Aggressive stance and barking with mouth open	"I'm not sure about you and I'm rather afraid and thinking about running away – best ignore me!"
	Lying on back and possibly passing dribbles of urine	"I give in – please don't hurt me!"
TAIL	45 degrees or more higher than spine	"I'm alert and interested"
	Clamped down over anus	"I'm rather nervous and afraid"
	Between legs and hind quarters crouched	"I'm really nervous and afraid"
	Tail gently waving	"I'm getting annoyed and thinking about being aggressive"
	Tail wagging	"I'm happy and enjoying myself"

CHAPTER 6

SOCIALISATION AND PUPPY DEVELOPMENT

1. How dogs learn
2. Stages of puppy development
3. Socialising your puppy
4. A dog's ambitions

Understanding how dogs learn is a fundamental necessity if you want a well-mannered dog that knows how to behave properly in society.

Learning is usually defined as a 'change in behaviour brought about as a result of previous experience'. Many texts on learning theory have been published, and, almost without exception, they contain much confusing terminology. New words are continually emerging and definitions change as the subject of animal behaviour is examined and discussed in ever greater detail. In the account below we have tried to simplify the situation by mainly using only words that are part of everyday speech and which most dog owners should understand. In the hope that it will be of additional help, the words we have used are defined, where they are not explained within the text, in the glossary at the back of this book (see Appendix One).

1. HOW DOGS LEARN
Essentially, dogs learn by habituation, socialisation, and association.

HABITUATION AND SOCIALISATION
• **Habituation:** acclimatisation to inanimate stimulae (sounds and objects).

- **Socialisation:** acclimatisation to animate stimulae (people and other animals).

As part of a survival strategy, nature ensures that newborn animals perceive all new experiences as being potentially threatening, and that they instinctively know that evasive action should be taken. Habituation means, in simple terms, 'the loss of such an unlearned, natural, inherent behaviour'. This comes about as the animal learns that the particular experience (stimulus) is not, after all, a cause for concern. For example, puppies are naturally fearful of loud noises and people emerging unexpectedly on their territory. However, if such noises or people are encountered every day, or at least frequently, without untoward result, the puppies will become 'accustomed' to them and ignore them. The natural response of fearfulness will be lost or at least reduced. This is how effective puppy habituation and socialisation works, and its importance will be obvious. If dogs are to fit into society, it is essential they learn that there is no need to be fearful of the noise of washing machines, vacuum cleaners, postmen, dustmen, etc.

Puppy socialisation classes have been set up in many areas of the country. Puppies are usually enrolled when they are between 12 and 18 weeks of age. These classes offer puppies the chance to learn 'doggy' body language from their peers. However, be aware that puppies attending these classes may think that all dogs, of whatever age, will want to be amenable and to play; they can be taken very much by surprise when that is not the case.

Nurses in many veterinary practices organise puppy parties. These can be helpful in respect of socialisation and provide the added benefit of providing owners with a good opportunity to obtain advice and meet like-minded people.

ASSOCIATION
Associative learning can involve:
- Conscious thought (in technical terms this is called instrumental conditioning).
- Involuntary reflex actions (this is called classical conditioning).

Instrumental conditioning
This is the main way that dogs learn. It simply means that a behaviour is determined by the result it brings. Or, put another way, dogs learn essentially by trial and error. By repetition, dogs learn that a certain action will bring a pleasurable experience or an unpleasant result. If the

result is pleasure, the dog learns that the action is worth repeating. If the result is painful or not pleasurable, the dog quickly learns that the action is not worth repeating since it does not 'pay off'! A dog will usually put its paw in the fire just once!

Dogs do not have the power of speech, and, therefore, they are unable to teach each other. As a result of this, dogs are unable to link a current situation with an event that happened some time ago. Consequently, a dog can only establish whether he has done right or wrong if his action brings a reward or 'punishment' within just 0.5-1 second. Understanding and appreciating the significance of this is fundamental if we are to modify a dog's behaviour and teach him to respond as we want to specific commands.

Even though humans can talk, it can still be just as difficult for us to link cause and effect when they are separated by a relatively long period of time. For example, our ancestors did not realise for years that sexual intercourse in humans was linked to giving birth nine months later!

When it is pointed out that, in order to be linked in a dog's mind, the action and the result need to occur within no more than a second of each other, some people erroneously think that dogs have short memories and can't think. But that is not the case. Dogs remember places, events, and, of course, their owners, even after a long period of time – possibly years! Dogs greet their owners like long-lost friends when collected from a boarding kennel after a long holiday. Dogs can and do 'think' and they can solve problems. If you play hide and seek with your dog, you will soon notice that he will look first in the hiding places you have used previously before he begins to search at random.

Classical conditioning

An example of this form of learning is the familiar experiment carried out with dogs by Russian physiologist Pavlov. He showed that salivation is an automatic reflex response whenever food comes into contact with the mouth. He went on to find that, if a bell is rung consistently at the same time as food is given, eventually dogs will learn that the sound of the bell heralds the receipt of food and they begin to salivate. They will do this to the sound of the bell even when food is not forthcoming. A more practical illustration of classical conditioning involves housetraining puppies. If puppies are taken outside when they are likely to want to go to the toilet (either to urinate or defecate) they will associate going out with the reflex body action. If, at the same time as the puppy 'performs', you whistle in an undulating way, the puppy will eventually 'learn' to urinate or defecate when he hears that particular whistle. Needless to say, such a prompt response can be very useful on cold, dark nights or when stops are made on a car journey! In the past, this method was used by grooms to encourage their equine charges to urinate outside the loose box, to minimise the need to 'muck out' or at least to make it easier. (For more information on housetraining, see Chapter Eight.)

2. STAGES OF PUPPY DEVELOPMENT

It is important to recognise that puppies go through a number of critical stages during their development. In particular, the first 12 weeks of life are of special importance. The stages and their duration are illustrated in the table below.

8. KEY STAGES OF PUPPY DEVELOPMENT													
STAGE OF DEVELOPMENT	WEEKS												
	1	2	3	4	5	6	7	8	9	10	11	12	13
Neonatal period	░	▓	▓	▓	░								
Primary habituation/ socialisation			░	▓	▓	▓	▓	░					
General habituation/ socialisation								░	▓	▓	▓	▓	░
Critical period for sensitivity								░	▓	▓	▓	▓	░

KEY

▓ Average start, end and duration of stage

░ These areas are included to take into account breed and individual puppy variations

Note: the duration of these events is variable between the breeds and individuals of the same breed.

NEONATAL PERIOD

This period occurs from two to four weeks of age, plus or minus one week. During this time, the pup is looked after principally by his mother. However, some interaction is needed by the breeder, mainly to ensure that all is well – that the puppy is sucking, urinating and defecating normally.

PRIMARY HABITUATION/SOCIALISATION PERIOD

This is the period between four and seven weeks of age, plus or minus one week. During this phase, it is important that the breeder begins to socialise (familiarise) the pup to being handled. This should be done purposefully and regularly, at least three to four times daily, from week three until the puppy goes to his new home. During this period the puppy should be further socialised by careful introductions to children in the house, selected adults, and possibly, potential purchasers.

During this primary phase, the pup should be habituated (accustomed) to the sounds he will encounter later in life, such as the sound of vacuum cleaners, dishwashers, carpet sweepers, the clatter of cutlery and crockery, the telephone ringing and the flushing of toilets, etc. It will be obvious that breeders have a big responsibility in this respect – their task being made much easier if the puppies are raised – at least initially – within the home. If this really is not possible, the use of sound CDs to prevent the development of sound phobias is worth considering (see Appendix Two).

During the latter part of the primary period, the breeder and the prospective owner should start the housetraining process (see Chapter Eight).

GENERAL HABITUATION/SOCIALISATION PERIOD

The period between eight to 12 weeks (plus or minus one week) is critical. In order to maximise development during this stage, it is advisable that puppies should go to their new homes as soon as possible after they have reached six weeks of age. Don't be concerned that the pups or the bitch will be any more upset by the earlier separation. The extra time your pup has with you as his 'mother' will be really advantageous later in his life. If owners wish to have an *ideal dog*, it is most important to use this phase to the full. It is at this stage that puppies are at the height of their learning ability.

Unfortunately, it is not always possible to obtain your puppy as early as six weeks of age, as licensed breeders are not allowed to rehome the puppies before eight weeks. Therefore, the onus is even more firmly on the breeder to begin the habituation and socialisation process between four and eight weeks of age, and onwards.

As soon as you have brought your new puppy hoome, you should continue to ensure that he is handled and introduced to all the situations, objects, machines, and people that he will be likely to meet throughout his life. He must be able to accept them happily. Some of the major objects, sounds and people to which puppies need to be socialised and habituated arc listed in the table below.

The all-important process of habituation and socialisation – which can make or mar the chance of the puppy becoming an *ideal dog* – requires much thought and dedication to ensure that each new experience is a happy one. There is the need to go slowly and carefully, and that is particularly the case during the critical period for sensitivity (see page 62). During this stage of a puppy's development, fearful experiences can be firmly imprinted for life. People should be introduced one at a time and then in groups of increasing numbers. The volume of sounds should be kept low initially.

9. SOUNDS, OBJECTS, PEOPLE AND SITUATIONS WITH WHICH DOGS SHOULD BE FAMILIARISED

PEOPLE	SOUNDS	OBJECTS	ANIMALS
Children playing loudly	Carpet sweepers	Balls	Cats and other pets
Crowded streets	Dishwashers	Bicycles	Cattle
Dustmen	Fireworks	Buses	Chickens
Joggers	Lorries reversing	Cars	Goats
Men and women (including vets!)	Police, fire and ambulance sirens	Lorries	Horses
People with sticks	Power tools	Post boxes	Other dogs
People carrying loads	Telephones	Phone boxes	Sheep
Postmen	Television/radio	Steps and stairways	Wild birds and wild animals
Rustling clothes	Vacuum cleaners	Trains	
	Washing machines	Traffic lights	

Although habituation and socialisation are particularly important between the ages of eight to 12 weeks, it should also, of course, be an ongoing process throughout the dog's early life. Remember also to accustom your puppy to everyday experiences, including walks in towns and the countryside, travel in various forms of transport, and even visits to your vet's surgery.

Finally, it must be stressed again that this time in a puppy's development is extremely important. In order to ensure that it can be used to the full, early vaccination against canine distemper, infectious canine hepatitis, leptospirosis and canine parvovirus infection is recommended. Ideally, the first vaccine should be given at six to eight weeks of age, and a second dose when the puppy is 10 to 12 weeks of age. However, the vaccination routine is dependent on the particular vaccine the veterinary surgeon recommends, and the incidence of disease in your particular area. Your vet will discuss this with you. For further information on vaccination, see Chapter Fourteen.

When you consult your vet about vaccination it is sensible also to seek his or her advice about worming your puppy. The introduction of modern worming compounds means that puppies can be wormed earlier in life – from two weeks of age! Again, your veterinary surgeon will recommend a product and a worming programme (see Chapter Fifteen).

CRITICAL PERIOD FOR SENSITIVITY

The critical period for sensitivity is between nine and 12 weeks of age (plus or minus one week). Any experience that causes acute fear at this stage may make the dog anxious, shy or very fearful of similar occurrences for the rest of his life. This is particularly likely to be the case with puppies that already have an introvert temperament. Dominant, extrovert dogs are much less likely to be affected in this way.

During the critical period, it is vitally important to avoid using punishment, or prolonged social isolation, to modify a puppy's behaviour. Also try to avoid, as far as possible, situations that you think might cause anxiety. For example, keep the puppy indoors with the radio or television on loudly if there is a thunderstorm or if fireworks are being let off (see also Chapter Twelve, under phobias).

If you are outside with your puppy and you hear a loud noise, such as a police car coming with its sirens going, distract your dog's attention by making him sit or obey some other command that he knows. Then reward him for a correct response with a tidbit and lavish praise. However, make sure that the dog does not 'think' you are in any way rewarding him for being fearful – that would be very counterproductive.

3. SOCIALISING YOUR PUPPY

As stated earlier, adequate habituation and socialisation is fundamental to the prevention of behaviour problems. We cannot overemphasise just how important this step is in creating an *ideal dog*. With an understanding of how dogs learn, and the stages of their development, it is possible to use this information to socialise your puppy to maximum effect.

NAMING YOUR DOG

If you haven't already decided on a name for your puppy, you need to do so. The sooner your pup becomes accustomed to his name, the easier training will be.

Choose a name that is short and snappy and that cannot be easily shortened or varied. It is best *not* to have an alternative affectionate name, as this can lead to confusion for your puppy. Ensure that everyone in your family realises the importance of calling the puppy by name at all times; this will greatly help the habituation, socialisation and training processes.

BASIC RULES AND TIPS

Listed below are some basic rules and tips that will help you to socialise your puppy without any problems.

- Plan ahead. Use your imagination, to try to understand what your puppy is thinking and experiencing, and you won't go far wrong.
- When he is forthcoming and shows no fear, always reward your puppy promptly with lavish praise and/or a tidbit. Speak in a kind voice, with feeling – "Well done!", "There's a good dog", etc.
- Make sure that you cover all contingencies, and particularly all sorts of people and other animals (see table 9 on page 61), one by one, during this critical time. Take special care that the puppy is not likely to be frightened by any new experiences.
- Habituate your puppy to the sounds and smells of towns and country, to suit your planned lifestyle.
- Make all new encounters cheerful and fun occasions, accompanied with lavish praise and jollying.
- Progress slowly and deliberately, and, if you sense an emerging problem, go back a step and work up again more slowly.
- Do not introduce more than two or three new experiences each day.
- Obtain an indoor dog crate or play-pen (see page 30-32) and give your puppy a suitably sized comfortable bed to which he can retreat. This will enable you to put the pup out of harm's way if you have to

leave him for a short while. The crate will also serve to keep the puppy away from temptations and avoid the need to have to correct any wrong-doing that occurred while your back was turned.

CARS

It is particularly important that your puppy becomes familiar with, and accustomed to, your car. Start by sitting in the front seat with your puppy on your lap. Make a fuss of him for about five miutes, on five to six consecutive days, while the car is stationary on the driveway with the engine turned off. Progress from this by getting your puppy used to sitting on the back seat or in the passenger footwell, and to the sound of the engine being started. Then try travelling a short distance, perhaps just around the block. Jolly the pup and reward calm behaviour with lavish praise and tidbits.

Dogs that become fearful, overexcited, or those that bark continually or suffer from car sickness are not just a nuisance but can be the cause of road traffic accidents. Aim to make your car a second home to your dog – a place where he can be left quietly on his own if necessary. If you have a secure drive, leave the car door open and let the puppy jump in and out on his own and sit on the back seat several times during consecutive days. Alternatively, let the puppy do this while you are present so that you can supervise the exercise. When the pup jumps in and sits or lies quietly, give lots of praise and a tidbit.

When you have trained your puppy to behave in this ideal way, teach him to wait quietly and calmly in the car on his own. Firstly, leave your pup shut in the car for only a very short time and observe him from a convenient hiding place nearby. This will allow you to return promptly if your dog shows signs of being anxious, or if he starts to behave inappropriately. Good behaviour should, of course, be lavishly rewarded on your return.

Gradually increase the duration of the time the dog is left until you're happy that he will be quiet and safe for at least the time it takes to do the week's shopping. By all means teach your dog to raise the alarm if someone touches the car, but do not encourage him to bark hysterically at people simply passing by.

It is extremely useful to be able to leave your dog safely in your car, without any anxiety on your behalf, for up to 1½ to 2 hours. To have a place where your dog can rest comfortably, out of the way, is particularly helpful when you have, for example, workmen in your house coming and going with tools and tins of paint, etc, or visitors who do not like dogs.

Whenever your dog is left in your car always ensure that:
- The car is not left in direct strong sunlight
- There is an adequate amount of ventilation by leaving the windows open an inch or two and that the sun roof, if you have one and the weather is suitable, is left open
- Your dog has access to water if he is possibly going to be left for more than 1½ hours
- There is no way that your dog can escape
- Your dog's lead is not left attached to his collar – it is only too easy for the lead to become caught around the handbrake or gear lever, which could choke your dog or see your car running away!

Dogs should never be left on their own in a car with children. Although they may be trustworthy as far as aggression towards children is concerned, they can cause serious injury simply by pacing actively, backwards and forwards if they fear that someone is going to invade 'their' territory or harm 'their' children.

When travelling with your dog *never* let him put his head out of the window. Not only is this dangerous, but you could end up having to seek veterinary help in respect of sore or damaged eyes.

PEOPLE

When introducing your dog to people, again, go slowly. First, use friends who are familiar with your house. Tell them, in advance of a visit, not to knock loudly on the door but to enter quietly. Ask them to speak to the dog, call him by name, and approach slowly, letting the puppy 'lead' the encounter as far as possible. If your puppy seems at all fearful, start by introducing him to newcomers from the safety of your arms. Jolly him along, praising the desired behaviour. Introduce quiet children one at a time, and, when successful, progress to noisy ones and bigger groups.

Anticipate the arrival of the postman and refuse collectors. Let your puppy hear the sounds they make, from the inside the house initially, with the doors and windows shut. During subsequent sessions, you can expose him to these exeriences a little more close by. Encourage these and other workmen to get to know your dog as a puppy. Again, get them to speak to your pup, calling him by name and letting him make the first moves. If such encounters are left until the dog is older and bigger, the workmen may show anxiety, which will inevitably be picked up by your dog, and the encounter can end up being totally counterproductive.

People walking with sticks, carrying loads and wearing clothes that rustle can all be cause for concern to a dog. They may possibly invoke a fear reaction in your puppy, leading to shyness of such sights and sounds, or even aggressive behaviour. Act out the situations and roles yourself before you let your puppy see strangers acting in these ways. When your puppy knows the meaning of **"Leave"**, teach him that chasing people on bicycles is not allowed and that obeying another learnt response is more rewarding.

OTHER ANIMALS

Introduce your puppy to other animals, particularly other dogs and cats. Go carefully and thoughtfully. Start with small dogs that are known to be friendly, and try to arrange the initial encounter on your territory. With cats it may be better to wait until your puppy has learned the meaning of the words **"Leave"** and **"Sit"** to avoid any chance of him realising that chasing cats can be fun and rewarding! It is better to introduce a cat to a puppy while you are in control – i.e. the puppy can be restrained while the cat is free to leave should she be alarmed by the puppy's presence. Work slowly, taking one step at a time.

When out for walks with your dog, and while he is learning about other animals, think ahead and cross the road if you see another dog approaching, especially if the dog looks as though he might be aggressive to your puppy. This will avoid any risk of conflict or a fear-invoking incident. Remember, prevention is your watchword – don't risk failure. When your dog is a little older, introduce him to known-to-be-friendly dogs. Joining training classes or puppy classes can be a useful way to accustom your dog to other dogs.

HANDLING AND GROOMING

As part of the socialisation programme it is particularly helpful to encourage all the members of the family to pick up, cuddle and fondle your puppy every time they see him when he is very young. Selected visitors should also be invited to do the same. This will ensure that your puppy is perfectly at ease and comfortable about being picked up in a variety of ways.

At this stage (starting at six or eight weeks of age), the person who will be mainly responsible for grooming your dog later in life should begin making plans and working out routines that will ensure that this job is done properly, regularly and with the least inconvenience. Apart from keeping your dog clean and looking great, grooming is an important part of the habituation and socialisation procedure. This is your chance to ensure that your dog will, in the future, not resent a close and full examination by anyone, including veterinary surgeons, should it be necessary.

Apart from these considerations, grooming reinforces your leadership role and will do much to ensure that you have an *ideal dog* that is obedient and happy in a subordinate role.

GROOMING TIPS

- Make grooming a regular procedure, carried out when you have an adequate amount of time available. Start with the young puppy when he is tired and relaxed after a period of play. Do not hurry the job, as the puppy must be taught that grooming is a pleasurable experience. Owners of older puppies and dogs may find that grooming is best done when the dog returns from his main daily walk and before he is fed.
- Select a place where flying hair and dust do not matter.
- Large dogs can be groomed standing on the floor, but for puppies and small- to medium-sized dogs, a bench or shelf at desk height, with a non-slip surface, can make the task much easier and safer.
- Purchase a good-quality stainless steel comb with round teeth inserted in the spine.
- Buy a good-quality natural bristle brush suitable for your dog's coat length. Use soft brushes for young puppies. Brush the puppy gently, for only a few minutes, following the way the hair lies. Breeders, pet shops and vets will give useful advice if you have any doubts.
- Have handy a small piece of 'J-cloth', flannel or cotton wool buds, so that you can wipe any discharge from the eyes or nose.
- Start by gently combing out any tangled or matted hair. Do not pull at any knots but carefully tease them out using a single tooth of the comb. This can be very uncomfortable for a dog, so don't be in a hurry. If the coat is very knotted or matted, use thinning scissors first to cut away part of the mat and then try using the comb again. Once all knots have been removed, proceed to comb and brush the whole coat. Don't forget to comb under your dog's neck, ears, collar, abdomen and his 'private parts'. Keep to the same routine every time you groom to ensure that no part is missed.
- Consider introducing regular weekly tooth brushing. Not only will this help to prevent gum and tooth problems in later life, it will also serve the purpose of accustoming your dog to having his mouth handled – this reinforces your leadership status and cements your bond with your dog. The staff at your veterinary surgery will help

advise you in respect of this matter and possibly supply a special dog toothbrush and paste to meet your needs; human toothpaste is not suitable. Products containing cetrimide are currently regarded as being best. These items can also be obtained from pet superstores or good pet shops.

- Pick up and stretch each leg in turn. Examine the paws, nails and pads for injury, and wash away any mud.
- If your puppy is of a breed that is traditionally clipped, it makes sense to accustom him to the sight, sound and feel of clippers, scissors and a hairdryer. Introduce him to these as soon as possible and while he is still young.
- Finally, always reward your puppy for submitting to being groomed without fear or resentment. Talk to your puppy during the procedure and make it a fun activity for both of you.

HEALTH CHECKS

When grooming your puppy, you should take the opportunity to give him a health check once a week.

- Look closely at both eyes. Check for any excessive discharge. The front of the eye should be clear and the inside of the eyelids should appear normal in colour.
- Lift the puppy's lip and open his mouth. Check the teeth, including the back molars. Note whether the teeth need cleaning, or if they are loose, and make sure that the gums are not inflamed. Puppies begin to cut their milk teeth quite naturally at about 14 days of age; there are no molars in this set. The milk teeth are usually shed and replaced by adult teeth by the time dogs are four to six months old. You probably won't see them go, but with the possible exception of the canine teeth, the temporary ones will not need extracting. If both temporary and permanent canine teeth are present, lying one behind the other, and the temporary tooth (the smaller and more transparent) cannot be removed easily, consult your vet. It can also be helpful, from health and behavioural points of view, to consider starting to brush your dog's teeth weekly. This will help to reinforce your status and also help to prevent gum disease.
- Check the ears, especially in the case of spaniels and breeds with floppy ears, for any foul-smelling discharge. Do not clean the sensitive inner parts of the ear by poking anything at all into it. Simply wipe the outer ear canal with a swab soaked in an ear-cleaning fluid available from your vet. If there is any persistent nasty smell from the ear, or a noxious dark-brown discharge, seek veterinary help.

- Check the dog's skin and coat. Feel for any abrasions or lumps. Pay particular attention to the abdomen.
- Ensure that the feet are not cut or that grit is caught in them. Also check that your puppy's claws are not too long. If your puppy resents a leg being lifted or a paw squeezed, this could indicate pain, so try to locate exactly where it hurts and what might be causing the trouble.
- Check the puppy's anus and penis/scrotum or vagina. Look for any signs of abnormal discharge. Be gentle with your puppy, especially when you first start such an examination. Dogs that allow such attention without fuss or fear can be a great help to vets if inspections of this sort are needed later in life.
- If anything untoward is found during your health check, consider whether or not a veterinary consultation is called for. In any case, make a note to keep an eye on the problem.

4. A DOG'S AMBITIONS

The majority of books on dog behaviour talk about dogs being pack animals. They often state that all dogs are programmed at birth to become top dog or bitch. To some extent, this is true, since it is nature's way of ensuring that the genes of the major achievers are inherited preferentially. However, what of those dogs that are not competitive? What of those that lack the drive, ambition, selfishness and the killer instinct necessary to get to the top of the heap? It is becoming clearer that many dogs do not have great aspirations; they are happy to stay as contented, relaxed 'servants', or just to be a member of the group, free from hassle and free of the need to struggle and make decisions. Others may be happy just to make a minor contribution to the group and climb a little way up the hierarchical ladder. In other words, dogs are, in a way, just like people. Some are willing to choose a more relaxed way of life, which means less responsibility and freedom from the need to compete. Some dogs are 'pushy', and some are more retiring and fearful. Some are extrovert and some introvert.

KNOW YOUR DOG

A dog's ambitions are of important relevance to all new puppy owners. They highlight the need to 'read' your puppy's body language, to assess his demeanour. You need to establish just how your pup is motivated, as this will affect your teaching approach.

Dominant, 'pushy' dogs will need to be taught, in no uncertain terms, that you, and all the members of your household that have regular contact with the dog, are in charge. Such a puppy needs to know that you expect him to be an obedient and supportive member of the group, one that can be trusted to carry out specific tasks for which he is ideally adapted and suited. Your status as the leader and decision maker, in the home and outside, must be continually reinforced. Adopt a strong, firm, unwavering attitude. Only give praise and rewards when you decide, make certain that you win all games (and end up in possession of all toys), eat first, and occupy the best seats and positions. (See also leadership/dominance exercises in Chapter Twelve.)

Shy or fearful dogs will need to be encouraged to socialise and play. Obviously, any strict punishment should not be used as a teaching method in such dogs. Instead, any wrongdoing is better being admonished by the temporary withdrawal of affection and privileges.

CHAPTER 7

TRAINING AIDS AND METHODS

1. Food
2. Praise
3. Punishment
4. Training devices
5. Reinforcing learned behaviour

I n simple terms, owners have three main aids or methods (tools) that can be used to teach dogs. If these are applied correctly and promptly, dogs will respond in the desired way surprisingly quickly.

1. FOOD

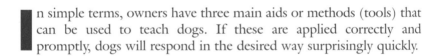

The use of small pieces of delectable food – a coveted tidbit, dog chocolate drops, pieces of meat or cheese – can be used very effectively as a reward for the desired response to a command. However, it should be noted that, since the reward needs to be given very promptly, wrapped food is of little use. The dog will not make the association between the command and his response if he has to wait for the reward to be unwrapped or retrieved from the depths of a coat pocket! Ensure that any food rewards you use are not given in such quantities as to unbalance your dog's diet. Do not use human chocolate, as this can be poisonous to dogs. Dog chocolate drops do not actually contain chocolate and can be used safely.

2. PRAISE

Any form of attention, including petting and stroking (especially if accompanied by verbal encouragement), will be regarded as praise by your puppy. As noted earlier, it is important not to praise your dog inadvertently when he is misbehaving. If this is done, the inappropriate behaviour will soon become part of the dog's repertoire. The most common example of this mistake is the owner who strokes and talks to a dog that is barking frantically when someone knocks at the door, in the hope that such an action will calm the dog. In fact, the dog will perceive the attention as praise or encouragement. In future, he will bark more loudly and for longer. In this connection, it is worth noting that acting over-sympathetically to a dog that is apprehensive can also be counter-productive. The action may be perceived by the dog as praise, encouragement, or at least attention, and he may think that being apprehensive is worth repeating as it 'pays off'.

3. PUNISHMENT

Punishment should be used only as a last resort, when reward-based methods have failed to achieve the desired results. There are occasions when punishment can be effective but for this to happen, it needs to be governed by some very important groundrules – it should be kept to a minimum, and it should never involve physical or mental cruelty.

ADMINISTRATION OF A PAINFUL STIMULUS

In this context, the severity of punishment will need to be varied according to the pet's size and temperament. This usually means a mild slap with your hand or the lead on the dog's body (but certainly not on the dog's head). Punishment of this nature must never be cruel, nor should it ever be used in temper.

Rather than resort to punishment, it is far better to give the dog a chance to adopt another learnt behaviour (which will bring reward) to replace the undesirable one. If punishment is used, try to follow the rules noted below.

WITHDRAWAL OF PRIVILEGES

Simply ignoring the dog, giving him no attention at all and showing your displeasure by your body language, will often be sufficient to teach the dog that there is no point in repeating the undesirable behaviour. If this is not enough, try banishing the dog to a room on his own and ignore him. In other words, social isolation for a short while can be extremely effective, and the dog will soon learn that the inappropriate behaviour does not 'pay off'.

MAGIC PUNISHMENT

So-called 'magic punishment' can be very effective indeed. A suitable object, such as a bean bag thrown from a hiding place, which strikes the dog while the crime is actually being committed, is particularly useful. This is because the dog does not link the punishment with the owner (the dog perceives that he is being punished by the environment).

This form of punishment is immediate and unpredictable. A single application of this method was sufficient to stop a Dobermann that had developed a habit of 'raiding' handbags left on the floor. This example highlights the value of 'set-up' situations, where the owner anticipates the wrongdoing and is prepared to administer punishment as the act is committed – there is no delay and the dog cannot help but make the association between cause and effect.

RULES GOVERNING THE USE OF PUNISHMENT

- Apply the punishment consistently and fairly and without delay.
- Make the punishment appropriate to the crime.
- Use punishment that is strong enough to disrupt the undesirable behaviour but which does not cause suffering or is prolonged.
- Do not punish shy, nervous dogs, or puppies less than 12 weeks of age. In such cases, a firm **"No"**, accompanied by disapproving body language, will usually be enough.
- A quick hard tap on the nose may be effective in the case of larger dogs, but care should be taken that such an action is not confused with play. this would be completely counterproductive and may even encourage aggression or anxiety.
- If you have any doubts about the appropriateness of punishment, it is better to ignore the behaviour. If in doubt, apply temporary social isolation.

4. TRAINING DEVICES

There are a number of training devices on the market, all aimed at making the process of training and socialising your dog a little easier. Some are more effective than others, although all work when used correctly and appropriately.

Do not be fooled into thinking that you *must* use these devices if you want a well-trained dog. While training devices can be useful tools in certain situations, an understanding of the way dogs learn, and how you can adapt that knowledge to suit your own particular puppy and lifestyle, is just as effective.

CLICKER TRAINING

Some dog behaviourists recommend clicker training when dogs are being taught to respond to commands. In essence, this method is an example of instrumental conditioning (see page 57), with the click acting as a positive secondary reinforcer. Using this method, the dog first learns to associate the two-toned click with getting a reward (a tidbit and/or praise). Once this connection is established, the clicker can be used to make the dog aware that his behaviour is correct, desirable and what the owner wants. If the method is to be effective, it is important to click while the behaviour is actually being done – not after it has been completed. Timing the click with precision is essential for success.

Clicker training works extremely well with dolphins, where giving prompt food rewards, petting and jollying are not options. One can only but admire what dolphin trainers can and have achieved. In the case of dogs, the pet learns to associate the sound of the click with getting a treat. All the owner needs to do is to click at the very instant the dog does something required. Very quickly the dog becomes 'tuned' into trying to make the owner click so that a reward is forthcoming.

However, while the effectiveness of clicker training is undoubted when used correctly, it can be difficult to apply this method to training dogs *in a family*. This is because clicker training requires an in-depth understanding of what is involved, split-second timing, and considerable dedication. It is difficult for clicker training to be easily undertaken and shared by all the members of a family. Furthermore, it is difficult to apply in dog training classes, where incessant clicking by several owners would serve only to confuse each individual dog.

That said, for someone with a scientific and enquiring mind, clicker training could provide an interesting and possibly rewarding experience. Diligently applied, it could allow such a person to train their dog to achieve virtually any action within his physical capability, with just a click. Working closely in this way will undoubtedly help to cement a very firm bond between the owner and their dog.

Another possible area where clicker training could be usefully employed is 'target training'. In other words, to teach the dog to draw your attention to some situation, such as the ringing of a doorbell or telephone. (For further information see Appendix Three.)

The rather more traditional training methods described in this book are simple, straightforward and they work. They have been tried and tested, and they are applicable in a family situation, allowing everyone in contact with the dog to be involved. By all means, if clicker training appeals to you, try it, but remember you can train your dog effectively without it.

TRAINING DISCS

Training discs can, theoretically, be used in two main ways.

- They can be thrown to the ground to distract a dog that is misbehaving, especially when he is out of reach, and so disrupt the behaviour. This rather limited use can be helpful in some cases, for example preventing jumping up or possibly chasing cats.
- The dog apparently seems to learn that the noise made by discs as they hit the ground is associated with an unwanted behaviour. The dog then goes on to associate the sound with the command **"No"** and eventually he will respond to the command **"No"** without the discs being employed. This, we consider to be an unnecessarily complicated, round-about and time-consuming way of teaching a dog simply to obey the spoken command **"No"**. However, if you are having problems getting your dog to obey your spoken commands, it is possible that training dics may help.

A bunch of keys, a tin filled with pebbles or marbles, a water pistol or a dog stop alarm can be used in a similar way to training discs. All these 'tools' have the disadvantage that they will not always be immediately available at the time of need. It is better and simpler to use a distinctive loud hand-clap together with a clearly spoken, sharp **"No"** if it becomes necessary to distract a dog's attention. This should be followed by giving the command for a learnt behaviour which allows the dog to 'escape' into a situation that will 'pay off'. If this approach is used from the word 'go' with a young puppy, very few problems should arise.

DETERRENT SPRAYS

A number of sprays containing citronella or another unpleasant smelling liquid are advocated by some behaviourists, particularly for young puppies, to prevent them chewing objects such as shoes or children's toys. They have also been advocated to help prevent dominant dogs from jumping up at people, including young children, and to aid the removal of a food bowl from a dog that is aggressive over food.

Sprays have several limitations, namely that they can teach the dog only to ignore items that have been sprayed. It is not possible to spray the shoes of all the people your dog could meet, nor is it feasible to spray all the children who come into contact with your dog! Do not use remote (spray) collars to control dominant/aggressive dogs. This can be dangerous and is certainly ill-advised. Such collars should be used only following one-to-one instruction from a trained and properly qualified dog behaviourist.

ELECTRONIC TRAINING DEVICES

These devices can be divided into two groups:
- Electronic containment devices
- Electric shock collars.

Both work on the basic principle of administering an electric shock to the dog, sometimes preceded by a warning buzz, to alter his behaviour.

Incorrect use of electric collars or electronic containment devices can, potentially, cause serious behaviour problems, such as fear and anxiety. Furthermore, if either device is maintained incorrectly, it could result in a serious burn or a significant, possibly even fatal, shock.

We are of the opinion that these devices are not suitable for use by the average dog owner. Indeed, we are minded to side with those people who consider that they should be banned or at least used only under licence by trained operators who have a proper understanding of dog behaviour.

PHEROMONE THERAPY

Dog appeasing pheromone (DAP) is a manufactured synthetic pheromone, delivered through an electronic 'plug-in' diffuser directly into the atmosphere, or more recently available as a spray product. It is aimed at reassuring dogs that suffer from stress or anxiety, as indicated commonly by panting, trembling, cowering, hiding, and seeking attention from their owner. DAP replicates the natural pheromone produced by the skin surrounding the mammary glands in lactating bitches and passed on to sucking puppies. Therefore, it encourages a feeling of well-being in the dog. It is claimed that destructive behaviour, excessive barking, house soiling and excessive licking can be reduced in severity. Furthermore, the product can be used to ease the strain of moving house, re-homing, visits to kennels or veterinary surgeries, in dogs suffering from separation anxiety, or those dogs with a fear of fireworks or possibly thunder. Your veterinary surgeon will advise whether the use of this product would be beneficial in your situation.

EXTINCTION

If you have any doubt about which training methods mentioned you should use when confronted with an undesirable behaviour, the best approach is to turn away and ignore the behaviour. It is far better to do nothing than to get it wrong. Relying on an inappropriate behaviour being extinguished (forgotten) is often a good safe option in many dogs and especially in those that have a tendency to dominance.

5. REINFORCING LEARNED BEHAVIOUR

An understanding of the way dogs think and learn, and an appreciation of the available teaching methods described in this chapter should allow you to work out for yourself what approach is ideal for your individual dog. The information provided, correctly applied, will enable you to prevent the establishment of undesirable behaviour in your dog and to 'train' him to respond properly and promptly to basic commands. As a result you will be able to mould your puppy quickly and effectively into a happy, contented *ideal dog* that fits snugly into your family group and into the community at large without causing friction. Bear in mind the following points during training and you should have few problems in establishing the behaviours you want.

- Learning is achieved more quickly if the response is rewarded (reinforced) every time a command is obeyed promptly and correctly.
- Intermittent, random, strong reinforcement (big rewards) are most effective in maintaining a desired behaviour. Think of the one-armed bandit, golf or fishing!
- If no rewards are given, the behaviour will extinguish – the response will be forgotten.
- If a reward becomes associated with a neutral stimulus (e.g. a sound, smell or visual stimulus that is of no significance to the dog), the stimulus can itself be used to reinforce a learnt behaviour. Such a stimulus is termed a secondary reinforcer. In clicker training the click becomes associated with a food reward thus allowing a desired response to be rewarded promptly through a click. Specific gestures can be used in a similar way but care must be taken that they are not used inadvertently to reward an inappropriate act by the dog.

CAUTION

As stated in Chapter Five, dogs are not clones, they are individuals. Just as a child's development will follow guidelines only loosely, the same is true with dogs. Be flexible in your approach to training. Too many dogs are spoilt by following regimented hard-and-fast rules.

However, while you should be flexible, there is no need to put up with unacceptable behaviour. Resolve to do something about it if you are unhappy. Do not turn a blind eye or make excuses. If you can't establish the cause of the problem, or your dog fails to respond to the course of action you decide on, seek professional help from a trained dog behaviourist or veterinary surgeon. If you have an aggressive dog, it is extremely important that you seek professional help.

CHAPTER 8

HOUSETRAINING

1. Different approaches
2. Tips for success

Housetraining can be a major cause of distress to the new puppy owner, but it does not have to be. While you should be prepared for accidents, you can largely prevent them from happening if you are diligent in your approach.

1. DIFFERENT APPROACHES

Many animal trainers recommend that puppies are taught to urinate and defecate on newspaper initially when introduced to their new home. They suggest that part of the floor in an indoor crate or play-pen is covered in newspaper and that newspaper also be put down near the outside door in the kitchen/utility room where the puppy is being raised. We feel, however, that this is messy and unnecessary and means that, at a later date, the puppy will need to be trained to 'go' off the newspaper, which doubles the task!

We feel that it is much better to 'go for broke' from 'square one'. While this may sound ambitious, it is a very realistic goal. If you are willing, able and dedicated enough, to monitor and supervise your puppy continually for the first five to seven days or so in your house, you can housetrain him surprisingly quickly. You can, of course, take 'time out' when the puppy is deeply asleep. Delegation to other members of the family is allowed, as long as they are also diligent and follow the set rules.

2. TIPS FOR SUCCESS

- Make up your mind that your puppy is not going to 'blot his copy book' – ever!
- Give your dog as much opportunity as possible to go to the toilet outside, and reduce his opportunities to soil in the house. Take him outside at least every 1½ hours during the day to begin with.
- Remember that your puppy will inevitably want to go to the toilet when he wakes up. If your puppy has had a snooze, take him outside straight away.
- Similarly, your puppy will want to relieve himself soon after a meal and possibly after a period of play. Be prepared to take your puppy outside as soon as he has finished eating, or when a period of play or excitement is over.
- Familiarise yourself with the signs your puppy will show when he is 'thinking' about going to the toilet. Usually, he will start by being restless, circle round and round, and finally begin to crouch. If you see these signs, or if you even suspect that the puppy is thinking of 'going', act promptly; take the puppy outside without delay, even if the phone rings – the caller will ring back if it is important!
- When your puppy 'performs' outside, make the undulating whistle mentioned on page 58, or any another command/phrase you prefer (such as "Be clean!"), to encourage him to urinate or defecate. Immediately the pup has finished, continue the whistle for a little longer and give lavish praise – verbally and by petting. If you can give a food reward *immediately*, do so. The puppy will soon learn to connect the whistle or command with going to the toilet, and this could prove very useful later on, when on journeys or in strange surroundings.
- We consider that it is not best practice to stick to one particular place or specific surface when encouraging your pup to go to the toilet outside. To do so could be counterproductive in the future, when the surface he is used to 'performing' on is not available. If you have trained your puppy to 'go' on grass or gravel alone, you could have a big problem if you stop at a motorway café or garage forecourt. It is better, from the start, to encourage your dog to 'go' on any surface, except, perhaps, the flowerbeds!
- Importantly, every member of your family must be prepared to take turns on 'puppy watch' and to follow the procedure you have adopted to the letter.
- Finally, if you happen to have a failure, do not chastise your puppy.

Simply mop up and resolve not to let it happen again. Because puppies will be naturally drawn back to areas where they have urinated or defecated previously, it makes sense to remove any scent from the area either using diluted biological detergent followed by spraying with spirit (provided that will not itself spoil the area), or by using one of the effective odour-eliminating products that are available these days. Remember that, because a puppy's sense of smell is far more acute than a human's, the smell may have been removed according to your nose, but not to your puppy's! If your pup can still smell the scent, he may chose to urinate/defecate in the same place, and then you will need to use a special pet-odour remover.

- Be positive – you will be surprised what progress you can make even in a few days.

CHAPTER 9

TRAINING EXERCISES

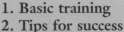

There is virtually no limit to what you and your dog can achieve. As long as you think like a dog and use the teaching methods described in Chapter Seven, your dog can learn to do, and enjoy, anything you want him to within his physical ability. Much fulfilment and a great sense of achievement is there for the taking – make the most of it!

Firstly, you will need to teach your dog to obey some essential basic commands, which are covered in this chapter. Once you have successfully established these, you can progress to more advanced training. Subsequently, you should ensure that your dog fits into present day society and provokes just admiration (see Chapter Ten). If you can make your dog into a fun-loving, happy subordinate, whose aim is to please at all times, to do as he is told, and to take part in the doggy activities you fancy, you will indeed have an *ideal dog*, and you can reap to the full all the rewards that dog ownership has to offer.

1. BASIC TRAINING
All dogs need to be trained to respond promptly and properly to at least six basic commands, namely:

• **Sit**
• **Down**

- **Stay**
- **Heel**
- **Come**
- **Leave.**

As you progress, you can, of course, add to these as you see fit – up to another five or six commands at first, and eventually even more. You should already have introduced the word **"No"** to indicate that you don't approve of what the puppy is doing. Your puppy should also be familiar with the undulating whistle used for housetraining (see pages 58 and 78) and the phrase "In your basket/bed" or similar (see page 29).

All commands should be given briskly and in a tone that demands obedience and prompt action. When asking/telling your dog to go to his bed, give the command in a more friendly way, and, at the same time, gesture towards the bed. Be sure not to use a tone that your dog may perceive as chastisement. Do not tell your dog to go to his bed as a punishment. His bed is his haven, where he can relax comfortably, quietly and undisturbed, away from any hustle and bustle. Your dog needs to enjoy being there.

2. TIPS FOR SUCCESS
Below are some general tips to help you achieve quick results in your training.
- Make training fun.
- Set aside three or four sessions each day during the crucial two months when the puppy is first in your care. Each session should last approximately five to 10 minutes, and each session should be devoted solely to formal basic training. Ideally, these periods should be between meals, and never just before you and your dog are due to go out for a walk or when he is anticipating an exciting happening. Dogs need to be able to concentrate.
- Some training can take place while your dog is out on a walk as suitable occasions occur. However, essentially, walks are exciting and for enjoyment, not for teaching basic commands. Your dog will be more interested in the surrounding smells and sounds, and will not be in a mood to concentrate. However, you can supplement lessons learnt in the basic training periods by getting your puppy to **"Sit"** at the curb side, for example, or to lie **"Down"** quietly if you meet a friend – but don't chat for long!
- It helps considerably, when you fist start training sessions, if you give a command as the dog is performing the action naturally. If you see

your puppy about to sit or lie down, say the relevant word, and, once he has completed the action, reward him immediately. Dogs soon cotton on that to obey 'pays off'.

- Use gestures *and* words. Motion your puppy into a sitting position, show the flat of your hand for **"Stay"**, and make a downward gesture for **"Down"**, etc. In the really fantastic obedience demonstrations at Crufts, the dogs work principally, if not entirely, from gestures by their handlers and their body language.

- Whatever words and gestures you adopt, don't vary them – ever. Make sure that everyone who has contact with the dog conforms precisely, every time.

- Make sure that a good, correct, prompt response to any command is rewarded with praise and/or a tidbit without delay. During the formal training sessions, make sure that you have any food rewards you wish to use close to hand. Once the response is learnt and well established, give rewards at random intervals to maintain the behaviour. However, never stop rewards altogether, as this can lead to the response being extinguished.

- Ensure that your dog does not jump up for food rewards; this can be an extremely annoying habit. If your pup does jump up, move away backwards, quickly saying **"No!"** and otherwise ignore the action. If your dog persists in trying to jump up, say **"No!"** and make sure that he can't achieve his objective by giving any future food rewards from a crouching position. Similarly, if your dog jumps up when greeting you when you arrive home in your car, welcome him from the car seat, instead of getting out straight away and giving him the chance to jump up. Ideally, you should first give your dog a learnt command, such as **"Sit"**, so that he has a desirable behaviour to 'escape to' that will bring a reward.

- As noted previously, always work towards preventing inappropriate behaviour. If you see your dog about to misbehave, distract him by giving a learnt command you can reward when obeyed. If in doubt, ignore any behaviour you don't approve of. Note, however, that if you decide to ignore a behaviour, you must do so consistently and every time. If you let it go even once in a while, your dog will try and try again to see if he can 'get away with it'.

- It is always useful to include your dog's name before or after the word of command – **"Rover, come!"** Using your dog's name will help to focus his attention on you.

- It is also a good idea to signal to your dog that the need to respond as requested is over by simply saying **"Okay"**.

3. SIT

Say **"Sit"** in a crisp way, and, as your dog begins to respond, offer a tidbit over his head to help ensure that he sits properly on the ground. If necessary, give a gentle, brief, downwards push on the base of his spine. Always reward promptly for a correctly completed response. Don't allow a 'half-sit' (the dog's bottom should be properly on the ground) or any delay in response. The aim is to get your dog to respond immediately and to stay there until you 'dismiss' him by saying **"Okay"**.

"Sit" is a particularly useful command, as it can be used to distract a dog that is misbehaving and thus save the need for chastisement. It is a useful behaviour that the dog can escape to if he has committed a misdemeanour.

4. DOWN

Give this command in a short, sharp voice, accompanied by a downward gesture of your hand. At first, you may need to start from the sitting position, and gently pull the dog's forelegs forwards, at the same time pressing him to the floor in the correct position. If your dog is not comfortable with that, it can help to encourage him into a Down position by kneeling and offering a tidbit from just above the ground. At first, reward your dog promptly every time he responds properly. Then, gradually increase the interval between the command and the

reward, so that the dog realises that he needs to stay in the **Down** position until you say **"Okay"** (brightly) and give him the reward. **"Okay"** is equivalent to the Army's **"At ease"** and it is a useful command that signals the end of a behavioural response to a command.

5. STAY

This is a really useful command should you happen to become separated from your dog, on the opposite sides of a road. Your dog must learn to obey this command promptly, whatever he is doing, whenever you see the need. The dog can remain still standing, sitting or in the **Down** position, until you tell him that it is **"Okay"** to move.

Say the word **"Stay"** in a sharp, urgent tone and hold up your hand with your palm pointing at the dog. Start with the dog close to you, so that you can reward him promptly. Then progressively increase the separation distance to 20 yards or more by walking backwards away from your dog.

6. HEEL

There is nothing more exhausting than a dog that pulls on the lead. Train your dog to walk closely to your left side, with his nose by your left leg, holding the lead loosely in your right hand. Remember to give the dog a chance to respond to the command **"Heel"** and then give a gentle tug on the lead if necessary – not the other way round. This can help to establish the behaviour. Eventually, you can reinforce the command silently if you tap your thigh lightly with your left hand as you say **"Heel"**. This sound and

gesture will reinforce and often eventually replace the need to say the word on every occasion. Keep changing direction as you walk along during a training session; this will help to prevent your dog pulling since he will be hesitant about what you are going to do next. If you are not making progress, consider obtaining a head/face collar, which may give you more control. If not, consider joining a training class or seek help from a trained dog behaviourist.

7. COME

Begin training your dog to respond to this command by using an extendible lead or the equivalent. Tell your dog to **"Sit"** and **"Stay"** and walk away backwards for a few paces. Then give the command **"Come"**, accompanied by an encouraging gesture towards yourself and possibly patting both your thighs. If your dog is reluctant to come to you, give a gentle tug on the lead. Always praise your dog when he comes to you and give him a tidbit. Ideally, you should encourage  the dog to come and sit in front of you. Always say the word **"Come"** in an encouraging, happy way.

As time passes, gradually increase the distance between you and your dog and let him stay sitting for increasing periods of time until you say **"Come"**. Do not forget to vary the places where training takes place. Teach your dog to **"Come"** in your garden, in fields, in woods, and anywhere you are likely to take him during the course of your lives together.

Eventually, if your dog has run too far away from you and you want him to return, first clap your hands to get his attention. This is better than shouting at the top of your voice, and it is also more effective; the dog will see your hands moving even from a distance, as well as hearing the clap. Then call him to you by saying **"Come"**. In the fullness of time, your dog may associate the hand clap with the word **"Come"** and always return to you when you clap your hands, which can, of course, be very useful. At the very least, this action will always serve as a cue to the dog that you need his attention.

If your puppy has been misbehaving in the distance, it can be useful to make him **Sit** and **Stay** before you call him to **"Come"**.

Never forget that you must always reward promptly a dog that comes quickly. Do not be tempted to shout **"Come"** in an angry voice if the dog does not obey straight away, and, when he does come, never ever scold or punish him.

8. LEAVE

Teaching your dog to **"Leave"** can be extremely useful in a number of situations. For example, if you see him about to pick up something unsavoury, or if he is looking a bit askance at another dog or a cat.

Start by saying **"Sit"**, and, instead of rewarding the action with a tidbit from your hand, drop the tidbit on the floor. At the same time, hold out your hand, with a finger pointed at the reward, and say **"Leave"**. After a second or two say **"Okay"** in a joyful voice and let your dog pick up the tidbit. Gradually increase the time interval between saying **"Leave"** and **"Okay"**. The dog will soon associate **"Leave"** with the action of not touching, especially if reinforced subsequently by throwing a ball or some toy on the ground and saying **"Leave"**. Your dog will quite quickly understand that **"Leave"** means "I must not touch anything".

9. CONSISTENCY OF TRAINING

While your puppy is learning all the commands noted in this chapter, it is probably best for just one member of the family to be involved in the training, so that it remains consistent. However, everyone who is in close contact with the dog should be kept 'up to speed' with what is happening, and all family members should follow precisely the method you have adopted. To help everyone, consider writing down the commands you use and 'post' them on the fridge or some prominent place.

By the age of 12 weeks, and certainly by 14 weeks of age, your puppy should be responding to all these commands and a number of others, particularly **"No!"** and **"In your bed"**. It will take some effort on your part to achieve this goal, but it will not be for long and it is well worthwhile. Remember that your puppy will learn much more quickly while he is young, so make the most of the first six to 12 weeks he is in your charge. However, make your expectations realistic – some dogs are quick learners, some learn more slowly. Be patient and don't think that you have failed if your dog is not quite as sharp as others – he may be a late developer!

CHAPTER 10

THE GOOD CITIZEN

1. Extended learning
2. Good manners
3. Causes for concern
4. Likes and dislikes

Although we have said that you should make good use of the first few weeks in your pup's life, that does not mean that your puppy's education stops then. Far from it! You should go on teaching your dog new commands throughout his life, partly for fun, partly through necessity, partly to exercise your dog's mind, and partly to continue to cement the bond between you and your pet.

1. EXTENDED LEARNING

Once you have mastered the basics of teaching your puppy (see Chapter Nine), you can extend the principles you have learnt to an almost-infinite variety of tasks and situations. If you see your puppy about to do something you like – offering his paw to hold, for example – give the action a name (e.g. say "Shake hands") and give your pup a reward. The response will soon be learnt because dogs will basically do anything, provided it pays off!

The sky's the limit, but go gently and slowly. Be determined not to make any mistakes, use plenty of praise, and make learning fun.

2. GOOD MANNERS

Teaching your dog to be well-mannered is extremely important in the world in which we live today. A

well-habituated and socialised dog should automatically be well mannered, but you should also use the teaching methods we have described to ensure that your dog fits the criteria noted in the 'profile' below. Don't hide behind excuses. If your dog is not behaving as you would like, resolve to do something about it by following the advice we give. Don't delay, start straight away. If the problem is serious and you can't cure it yourself by applying our principles, seek help from a trained animal behaviourist.

You may also like to consider enrolling on the Canine Good Citizen Scheme, run by the Kennel Club. There are various levels of classes, each becoming progressively more difficult. The scheme covers most of the desirable behaviours discussed in this chapter and the previous chapter. For details about classes in your area, contact the Kennel Club (see Appendix Two).

---

10. PROFILE OF A CANINE GOOD CITIZEN

An *ideal dog*:

- Obeys commands promptly
- Walks sedately to heel without pulling
- Waits patiently while you talk to friends when on a walk
- Likes to meet new people and be fussed and admired
- Loves regular walks
- Appreciates love and affection and being part of the family
- Enjoys fun and playing games
- Likes to retire to a comfortable bed
- Enjoys riding in the car
- Is happy to be left alone in the car or house for a reasonable length of time
- Likes being groomed daily
- Is happy to spend time in kennels
- Is fond of children and can be trusted around them
- Is well behaved with other dogs
- Is happy to have a full health check by you and the vet
- Is a deterrent to intruders
- Knows the house rules and obeys them

---

3. CAUSES FOR CONCERN

If your dog begins exhibiting any of the following behaviours, you need to take steps to stop it, before the behaviour becomes established. If this happens to you, return to the basics covered in Chapters Seven to Nine, remembering that preventing your dog from having the chance to commit the 'sin' is far more effective than punishing him once the sin has been committed. If you feel out of your depth, consult a professional.

Your dog should not:
- Jump up at people
- Bark hysterically when someone passes the house or car
- Chase people, cyclists, cats or cars
- Territory mark in the house
- Beg for tidbits
- Run away, whatever the provocation
- Show aggression to people or other dogs
- Pull on the lead
- Lick people's hands or faces
- Eat his own faeces or those of other animals
- Attempt to mount inanimate objects or people
- Even think about biting people, attacking other dogs or soiling in the house
- Mind visiting the vet
- Be destructive in the house or car
- Be unruly
- Be disobedient
- Be overtly oversexed
- Be overly submissive or shy
- Be dominant and aggressive
- Be frightened by the noise of washing machines and other appliances
- Be fearful of, or aggressive to, dustmen, postmen, etc.

4. LIKES AND DISLIKES

We ask a lot of our dogs in our attempts to get them to adapt to our human way of life. Generally, dogs are only too willing to try to please. Think about life from your dog's point of view and try to return the favour.
The following likes and dislikes should give you some idea of how to reward your dog's good behaviour as part of everyday life.

LIKES
- To be petted, loved and a part of the family.
- Receiving tidbits when he has been obedient.
- Playing games, fetching balls and playing hide-and-seek.
- Showing off how obedient he is by responding quickly to commands. Impress your visitors!
- His bed and knows it is a place where he can be quiet and relax. Do not allow him to be disturbed when he is resting.
- Being groomed regularly each day.
- Going for trips in the car, especially if it entails a new walk or somewhere where swimming is possible.
- Visiting food shops (but knows it's not allowed).
- Knowing the house rules and where he stands. An *ideal dog* would, no doubt, like the opportunity to go upstairs and sit or lie on the furniture, but he knows that it is not allowed, and accepts the situation with good grace.
- To behave well in other people's housees when visiting them.

DISLIKES
- Being separated from his family, but is happy to be left in boarding kennels, knowing that it will not be long before he is reunited with his family.
- Being left at home alone, but knows that someone will return in no more than three to four hours.
- People who ignore *ideal dogs*.
- Being shut away when people are eating (but knows why it is done).
- Not knowing the ground rules and what behaviour is expected and accepted.
- Being dirty and having a tangled coat.
- Having to go to the toilet in an emergency in an inappropriate place.
- Not wearing a collar.
- People who pull or jerk on the lead.
- Being left to exercise alone.
- Upsetting anyone in the family by behaving badly.

CHAPTER 11

PLAY AND ACTIVITIES

Like ourselves, a puppy's life is for living. It should be fun. Like you, your puppy wants to enjoy life; he does not want only to work, being rewarded or chastised by rote. Furthermore, dogs are there to be enjoyed by us, and much of that enjoyment comes from playing games together.

1. THE IMPORTANCE OF PLAY
Playing with dogs is fun. It helps to use up some of your dog's excess energy and also allows you to reinforce some of the basic commands and cement the relationship between you and your pet.

2. BALL GAMES
Instinctively, almost, we throw balls for dogs to retrieve. Dogs very obviously enjoy this game and soon learn to anticipate what the ball will do so they can get to it and catch it. Make sure you teach your dog that it pays to bring the ball back so that you can throw it again. Train your dog to drop the ball at your feet or allow you to take it from his mouth without objection. Many a dog will tease his owner by playing hard to get! Just as you reach out to get the ball it will be snatched away by the dog.

Don't be tempted to play that game, for the dog is bound to win if he wishes!

3. HIDE-AND-SEEK

We enjoy watching dogs play hide-and-seek with us or searching out food rewards or hidden objects. Use the words "Find it!" Dogs clearly enjoy exercising their minds as well as their bodies and it pays to create ways to make your dog think and work things out. Be inventive. Look at the things your dog is good at doing and encourage such activity with rewards and praise.

4. ROUGH-AND-TUMBLE GAMES

A word of warning – never, ever play tug-of-war games with any dog that has a guarding instinct, such as Bull Terriers. It can so easily imprint aggression. In this context, also make certain that any rough-and-tumble games are stopped when you are winning. If you even look like losing, call a time out, stop the game altogether and wait until another day, under changed rules!

5. TWO'S COMPANY

Try letting your dog run with another, known-to-be-well-behaved dog belonging to a friend – the energy expended in this way is considerable, more than can be achieved with you and your dog on your own.

6. PIG IN THE MIDDLE

Dogs love to play 'pig in the middle' because they can run backwards and forwards between the two people who are taking part, and show off just how high they can jump. Teach your dog to catch a ball or a frisbee, but nothing hard – teeth can so easily become broken. Call your dog back and forth between two members of family. Also consider setting up a hoop for your dog to jump through, or a scramble board to climb over. If your dog shows signs of excelling at games of this sort, consider teaching him flyball, or taking him to agility classes, which will exercise both the dog's mind and body and give you a new interest.

There are two points to consider carefully when playing active games with your dog that involve jumping. Firstly, beware you are not teaching escape behaviour! Secondly, you should never allow your dog to play jumping games until he has finished growing, or you could end up damaging his vulnerable puppy joints and ligaments.

7. FURTHER ACTIVITIES WITH DOGS

There are many other activities that you can enjoy with your dog, which will serve also to cement the relationship between you and your pet. A useful starting place is to join a local canine breed or training club. You may wish to consider some of the activities listed below.

• Showing
• Competitive obedience
• Agility
• Flyball
• Tracking
• Charity events involving dogs, e.g. sponsored walks
• Field and working trials (for working dogs)
• Therapy work (visiting old people's homes, hospitals, schools, etc.).

Consider joining the Kennel Club's Good Citizen Dog Scheme or Companion Dog Club, which are open to owners of crossbreed dogs or non-registered pedigree dogs. The Good Citizen scheme is designed to help owners train their dog to be obedient in everyday situations. It is not competitive and is aimed at all dogs, pedigree and crossbreed, regardless of age. Puppy training can begin from as early as 12 weeks old. For more details and a full list of local training organisations contact the Kennel Club (see Appendix Two). Ideally you should check out a number of training clubs in your area to pick the one that is most appropriate to your needs, particularly in respect of the advocated training methods and the type of people it attracts.

The Kennel Club has also set up The Young Kennel Club especially for young dog lovers between eight and 25 years of age. For further details contact the Kennel Club (see Appendix Two).

Finally, check your local paper for advertisements and reports on 'doggy' matters. Talk to like-minded people as you walk your dog. Consider joining your local canine club. All these options could open a whole new world and way of life for you and your pet.

CHAPTER 12

OVERCOMING PROBLEMS

1. Solving common behaviour problems
2. Dominance and oversubmissiveness
3. Aggression
4. Separation anxiety
5. Phobias
6. Seeking additional help

By following our advice, most owners will have no problems raising an *ideal dog*, and they will have the sense of achievement that goes with that. However, occasionally, owners will encounter some areas of difficulty and it can be helpful to seek advice from a trained dog behaviourist or to join socialisation or dog training classes. This can have the advantages that an experienced outsider may more easily identify what is going wrong, there will be the chance to meet other dogs, and, importantly, other owners; the exchange of views and experiences can often be very helpful. Do make sure, however, that any class you join is run by someone who you can relate to and who does not advocate an aggressive, dictatorial approach to training. Plans are currently being made for dog trainers to have undergone recognised training and to have relevant recognised certification. When this happens, your choice will be made much easier.

1. SOLVING COMMON BEHAVIOUR PROBLEMS

Even if you have done everything right during training, it is possible that your otherwise *ideal dog* will adopt some undesirable behaviour. If that should happen, use your newly acquired knowledge in respect of how dogs think and learn, and the methods by which dog behaviour can be shaped, to overcome the problem. You should, very often, be able to 'do it yourself'. Start by considering the questions noted below. Hopefully, if these are answered truthfully, this will allow you to identify the cause, and, as a result, the solution will become clear.

IDENTIFYING THE CAUSE
- **Step 1:** Try to identify the cause of the problem by analysing the situation carefully. What exactly does the dog do? Does the behaviour occur regularly, apparently at random, or is it associated with some specific event? For how long has it been going on? Have you recently changed any routine? Is the dog left on his own more frequently or for longer periods of time than previously? Are you at home less often, maybe as a result of becoming employed or through a change of job? Has there been any other change to family life, such as the arrival of another pet or a new baby?
- **Step 2:** Examine your attitude to your dog and that of everyone else who has regular contact with him. Are you, or someone else, inadvertently rewarding the dog when he behaves in a way you don't approve of? Remember that most dogs regard any attention as praise, even though it may be intended as chastisement or firm punishment!
- **Step 3:** Consider whether, as a result of leniency or insufficient attention, your dog has become too dominant and too pushy. Is someone applying inappropriate punishment or being too liberal with tidbits and favours? Could the problem be sexually motivated in the case of male dogs? Have some corrective procedures already been applied and failed? Were they really appropriate?
- **Step 4:** Once the cause has been identified, make the necessary change(s) and an action plan for everyone involved with the dog, to overcome the problem and prevent the situation occurring again.

TAKING ACTION
Table 11 opposite lists some of the common behaviour problems that can arise and gives some guidance and tips on what action can be taken to try to remedy the situation. If the suggested solutions do not bring a quick response, seek the help of your veterinary surgeon or a qualified dog behaviour consultant. The behaviour will become more deeply imprinted, and more difficult to cure, if there is a long delay before obtaining help. Finally, don't be tempted to take advice from 'a man in the pub', or some casual acquaintance, who may say that they have experienced the 'same thing'. Every case, every owner, and every dog is unique and generally requires a specifically tailored remedy.

11. SOLVING COMMON BEHAVIOUR PROBLEMS	
BEHAVIOUR PROBLEM	INITIAL REMEDIAL ACTION
Excessive barking	Never encourage barking by saying things such as "What's that?" in an excited voice when a noise is heard. Ignore the dog when he barks and make no physical contact with him at all; to do so could be regarded by the dog as praise. Make sure that the dog is not being left on his own frequently or for too long. If the dog is left alone, leave the radio on. If the dog barks in your presence, give the command **"Down"** and say "Be quiet". Reward him for obeying promptly. The objective is to teach the dog that lying down quietly 'pays off', whereas barking does not – barking from a lying position is difficult.
Biting – nipping at hands and ankles	Say a sharp "No" and/or give mild punishment as the crime is committed, followed by social isolation and the withdrawal of favours – the behaviour should extinguish. Reinstate basic training exercises and start carrying out the leadership/dominance exercises described later to ensure that your dog knows that *you* are in charge.
Excessive chewing	Only give your puppy one or two specific objects to chew (e.g. a special toy or raw-hide chews). If your dog goes to chew something else, distract him with a command, such as **"Sit"**, and praise him for responding properly. Substitute the chewed item with an acceptable object. Make a determined effort to remove all temptation in the future. This problem is one that lends itself to be cured by 'magic punishment' (see page 73).

SOLVING COMMON BEHAVIOUR PROBLEMS	
BEHAVIOUR PROBLEM	**INITIAL REMEDIAL ACTION**
Aggression towards people	Seek professional help. Sometimes such aggression can be stopped but it is vital to establish and eliminate the cause, possibly pain, fear or simply excessive dominance or over-guarding behaviour. If this is not done properly, the dog may never be trustworthy in this respect. If you have young children in your house or nearby, take extra care and be prepared for the fact that your dog may need to be destroyed.
Hypersexuality in male dogs including:- • Aggression • Mounting inanimate objects and people • Territory marking about the home • Roaming • Destruction • Excitability	Make sure that you are not inadvertently reinforcing the behaviour. Remove temptations and opportunity, and ensure that your property is properly fenced. Give your dog plenty of physical and mental exercise. Consult your veterinary surgeon. In dogs that have not yet reached adolescence, behaviour training methods, possibly coupled with medication, may be successful. In adult dogs, chemical or surgical castration can be of help, perhaps combined with other medical treatment. There is no need to 'put up with' such behaviour in most cases!
Jealousy between dogs	Enhance your leadership position over both dogs. The situation can be helped by increasing the status of the more dominant dog, (although it may not sound very British!) with the objective of encouraging the underdog to accept his subservient role, and, therefore, be more contented and comfortable. The dominant dog should be fed first, given more attention, and receive more favours.

SOLVING COMMON BEHAVIOUR PROBLEMS	
BEHAVIOUR PROBLEM	INITIAL REMEDIAL ACTION
Jumping up	Try to stop this behaviour through extinction. When the dog jumps up, quickly turn away with arms folded and ignore him. If you can see the warning signs, quickly tell your puppy to **"Sit"** and then reward him. Apply this consistently and your pup should soon learn that he receives attention only when he is sitting quietly.
Chasing people and animals	Spend as much time as you can on obedience training. Make sure your dog responds properly and promptly. Concentrate on the command **"Come"**. Carry out the leadership/dominance exercises described on pages 101-102. Use a thrown object, a jet of water or training discs to distract the dog and stop him as he takes off. Use a 'set up' situation so that you can use 'magic punishment'.
Submissive urination	Build up your dog's confidence by giving him some privileges and letting him begin to lead (see page 101).
Aggression towards other dogs	Avoid contact with other dogs wherever possible except those that are known to be friendly, and build up gradually. If, on a walk, a dog is seen in the distance, cross to the other side of the road and start giving the command **"Leave"** as early as possible followed by **"Sit"** and **"Stay"**, accompanied by an appropriate hand gesture. Make the dog look at you to distract him, and reward him for being quiet as the other dog passes. In male dogs chemical or surgical castration may help in some persistent cases – your vet will advise.

SOLVING COMMON BEHAVIOUR PROBLEMS	
BEHAVIOUR PROBLEM	INITIAL REMEDIAL ACTION
Disobedience	Increase your leadership status and reinstate formal basic command training exercises. If in doubt about what action is appropriate, walk away and ignore the situation.
Car sickness	Dogs can suffer from true motion sickness. If so, you will need to obtain suitable medication from your veterinary surgeon. Most frequently, however, car sickness stems from anxiety on the part of the dog, possibly as a result of a previous bad experience. Some cars may be more inclined to make dogs sick than others, and this can be worth checking before any other action is taken. Otherwise accustom the dog to the car whilst it is stationary in the drive-way, and let him get in and out freely. Provide your dog with a comfortable cushion on the back seat. Once the dog is happy, let him go in the car after a long tiring walk and just drive round the block. As long as the dog is happy and relaxed, increase the distance covered gradually. If the dog drools or whines, ignore him completely – next time reduce the distance and start again. Make sure that initial trips in the car are enjoyable, ending up with a walk at a favourite place.
Eating own faeces (coprophagy) or those of other animals	Remove temptation by picking up promptly any faeces in the garden. Watch your dog closely when walking in fields. Use the **"Leave"** command if he even looks at such matter. Call **"Come"**, command **"Sit"** and reward your dog when he responds correctly. Take with you a suitable object, such as a bean bag, to throw at your dog if he is some distance away and shout **"No"** as he is about to eat the offending material. Your dog should soon learn that such an action most certainly does not 'pay off'!

2. DOMINANCE AND OVERSUBMISSIVENESS

If you have thoroughly socialised and habituated your dog, you should have little trouble with him being too dominant. Your dog should respect you as the 'leader', knowing that you are in charge, that people go through doorways first, and that humans have exclusive use of the  bedroom and, if you decide, the whole of the upstairs part of the house. Your dog should know that there is only one set of rules in your house – yours!

It is very important to teach your dog not to be at all possessive over food, chews, bones or toys. Your pup must learn that you give such things and that you are also entitled to take them away. Try not to let any such confrontations arise. If you see a situation developing, lure your dog away with something more tasty and exciting, and then remove the original object while he is distracted. You can then give the object back when you decide.

However, some puppies are extroverts and pushy, and others tend to be introverted and shy. Occasionally, the former can become temperamental, and, in big guard dogs, that can become a problem. If you think this is happening, start to carry out the leadership/dominance exercises described below. Continue with them regularly, once or twice a week, until you have no cause for concern. Subsequently, do the exercises occasionally, perhaps just once or twice a month.

On the other hand, you may consider that your dog is too submissive. Perhaps he lies on his back in front of you, exposing his abdomen. Perhaps he urinates involuntarily, when he thinks you are cross or even just unhappy with his behaviour. You can boost the confidence of such dogs by allowing them to put their fore legs on your shoulders, briefly, when you are in a kneeling or crouching position, and also giving him a few extra privileges. You should also consistently and actively ignore the dog when submissive postures are adopted. You can, furthermore, respond very promptly when your dog wants you to make a fuss of him. Respond very positively when he wants to take the lead, or, as the saying goes, begins to occupy some of the 'high ground'. But don't go too far, – you must still remain the boss.

LEADERSHIP/DOMINANCE EXERCISES

The exercises noted below are intended mainly to reinforce your position as the pack leader. They have been used for many years and are known to be effective. They follow very much what the puppy's mother did when the pups were very young.

FIGURE 12.
EXERCISES FOR ASSERTING DOMINANCE

Dominance method 1

Dominance method 2

- Stand over the dog from behind, lift his front legs off the ground and keep them off the ground for 30-45 seconds. Reward the dog with spoken praise if he remains still and quiet, but rebuke any struggling (see Dominance method 1).
- Place the dog on his side and hold him there with one hand on his muzzle, keeping his mouth shut and the other pressing down firmly on his chest. Hold him in that position for 30-45 seconds and give praise or rebuke the dog verbally as appropriate (see Dominance method 2).
- Reinstate or step up the basic training exercises (see Chapter Eight). Be very particular that the dog responds quickly and properly to the basic commands. Do not tolerate any hesitation. Reward good behaviour lavishly.
- Finally, ignore the dog if he begs in any way, or seeks praise when it has not been earned. Turn your back meaningfully, don't say a word. Do this every time. If you are not consistent, the dog will certainly try it on again in the hope that you may respond again favourably by giving some attention, which he will perceive as praise!

3. PREVENTING AGGRESSION

Aggression is a major cause of owners having their dogs 'put down'. If your dog ever bites someone or is threatening children, seek advice promptly from

your vet or a qualified animal behaviourist and be prepared for the fact that euthanasia may be the only answer. People's safety must be paramount – never underestimate the situation or hide behind excuses. The next time could be a disaster.

Prevention is particularly important. You should, from an early age, take the precautions and actions noted below to ensure that your dog would not even think about behaving in this way.

- Do not play tug-of-war games with your dog – ever.
- Do not play boisterous games with larger, more extrovert dogs and particularly with dogs bred for guarding, such as German Shepherds or Dobermanns.
- Chewing acceptable objects is allowed but should be stopped if it becomes excessive.
- Biting, snapping or nipping with the front teeth is not allowed on any occasion. Hands are not for biting and neither are feet.
- If your dog does start such actions, say a sharp **"No"**. Show your displeasure and ignore the dog for a while. Consider giving the dog the chance to 'escape' into an acceptable learnt behaviour. If more severe, put the dog in a room on his own for 15 to 20 minutes. Importantly, make sure that you, or anyone else in the house, does not give the dog the opportunity to repeat the behaviour.
- Finally, step up the basic training lessons and carry out leadership/ dominance exercises frequently (maybe two or three times a day) and regularly. Do everything you can to ensure that your dog knows that you are in charge. If necessary, withdraw any favours for a while.

4. PREVENTING SEPARATION ANXIETY

It is very important that you are able to leave your dog in the house or in your car on his own, knowing that he will stay quietly and without causing any damage, such as scratching at doors, tearing seats, and trying to escape.

Destructive behaviour is, sadly, one of the most common reasons for dogs being sent to a rescue centre or being 'put down'. It is quite incredible just how much damage a dog can do in a kitchen or a car in a very short period of time. Because of these facts, it is essential to take steps early in your pup's life to prevent this happening. If you follow the procedure noted below, you should be able to leave your dog for short periods, confident in the knowledge that you will not be faced with a scene of devastation when you return.

- Start when your puppy is small – about 12 to 14 weeks of age is ideal.
- Make sure that your dog is used to, and comfortable in, his bed in the

house, or on a cushion or a bean bag on the back seat of your car, when you are present. The bed can be in a dog crate, if you are using one.

- Ensure that your dog is tired and not hungry, so that he is more inclined to sleep, and that he has been taken out to relieve himself.
- Decide on a specific action you are going to take in the future when you leave your dog alone in the house, such as turning on the radio softly, turning on a low light, or giving your dog a favourite toy that is kept for this purpose only. This action will serve as a valuable cue to the dog that you will inevitably return, albeit after a variable period of time. Make sure that you perform this pattern each and every time you go out.
- Make sure that your dog has access to water, that the place is adequately ventilated, and that he is not likely to get cold or too warm.
- As you leave, talk to your dog in a normal voice, saying things like "There's a good dog" and "Won't be long", and give him a quick pat. Although the dog will not understand the words, he will soon recognise the tone and the way you say it, which will reinforce the dog's understanding that you will return. Try not to vary in any way what you do and say; consistency is very important. You may, if you like, give your dog a small treat, such as half a sweet biscuit, as you leave.
- Start by leaving your dog for a very short period, perhaps as little as five minutes, making sure your dog has noted the adopted cue. Don't go far, keep out of sight and preferably remain within earshot. If all is well on your return and you have not heard your dog bark or whine in your absence, reward your dog with a favourite tidbit and give lavish verbal praise, telling him that he has been a 'good dog'.
- Over the next seven to 14 days, gradually increase the interval that you are absent for by five to 10 minutes at a time, eventually working up to two hours. Initially, it is sensible to wait somewhere out of your dog's sight but from where you can see and hear him, so that you can return promptly should your dog start to bark, whine or become excitable. Should that happen, go back, ignore the behaviour, settle the dog down and go through the chosen procedure. However, leave the dog for a shorter period of time and start to lengthen the separation period more gradually.
- Finally, if you aim to make up to eight such 'practice' departures over two to three days, you will, provided you have no failures on the way, be able to leave your dog safely for at least an hour in less than a week. However, do not set your expectations too high; it may result in you hurrying the procedure too much.

5. PHOBIAS

Dogs that develop a phobia pose a real worry to their owners. A phobia may involve an excessive fear of certain stimulae, such as noises, flashes of light, people, or unusual objects. Such a response can lead to serious injury to the animal and sometimes his owner or other people. Furthermore, much damage to property can result from the frantic attempts by the affected dog to 'escape'. It seems that sound phobias, particularly to fireworks, thunderstorms and traffic noise, are common these days.

Dogs that have undergone careful and comprehensive habituation and socialisation should not have an excessive fear response to everyday stimulae. However, it is not always possible to cover all eventualities and it is not uncommon for some dogs, especially those of an introvert nature, to develop exaggerated signs of stress or anxiety in unusual situations, such as during thunderstorms or when fireworks are being let off. It is, in fact, now considered that excessive fearfulness is a trait that can be inherited, although it is also the case that such behaviour may be the result of inappropriate actions by the owner. This is often the case in respect of fireworks, since if a dog shivers and shakes when loud sounds are accompanied by flashes of light, the natural instinct of the owner is likely to be to pet and cuddle the dog. This will inevitably be 'read' by the dog as a reward or praise and it will, as a result, continue to shake and shiver to an even greater extent on future occasions.

It will be obvious that many phobias can be prevented by thinking ahead, careful habituation and socialisation, and by thoughtful response by the owner when signs of fear are shown. If that fails, it will be necessary to think in terms of treatment as short-term management and, importantly, to use behaviour modification techniques to prevent problems in the future.

SHORT-TERM MANAGEMENT

If your dog shows signs of phobia for the first time, such as during a thunderstorm or when fireworks are being let off, it is worthwhile trying the following procedure if your dog's reaction is not too severe.

- As soon as your dog starts to shiver, shake and pace about the house, shut the doors and windows and draw the curtains. Take your dog into the lounge and turn on the TV or radio as loudly as you can stand to mask the noise outside as much as possible.
- Do not fuss, try to calm, touch or pay any attention to your dog. He may perceive your actions as praise, which would be very counter-productive. Dogs only too readily pick up human emotions; so it is

important that everyone in the household makes a big effort to stay calm.
- If it is necessary to take your dog outside to go to the toilet, be sure to keep him on the lead. Do not leave him unattended, even for a minute, because, in his panic, he may well take off and become lost.
- Once the noise starts to decrease and your dog begins to relax, go through a few behaviour exercises and reward lavishly a good, correct response. Many behaviourists consider that it is better not to take this action as the sounds start, as it might just serve to draw attention to the fear-evoking stimulus.

If your dog has reacted badly to noise in the past, think about a plan of action that you can adopt should the need arise again. Generally, it is a good idea to provide the dog, in advance, with a den or bolt hole where he can be seen and where he will feel safe and can stay until the noise and flashes stop. By and large, you will be more successful if you let the dog choose where he wants to go for himself – under a table, in a cupboard, or whatever. If this proves unsuccessful, consult your vet. In some cases you may be advised to use dog appeasing pheromone, known as DAP (see page 76), before your dog becomes agitated and while the sounds are going on. In some cases, vets will advise that your dog is dosed with anxyolytic drugs (compounds that reduce anxiety) or sedatives; sometimes these drugs will be prescribed in combination.

LONG-TERM MANAGEMENT
As in many cases of inappropriate behaviour, prevention is far better than attempted cure. This is particularly so in the case of firework phobia. These days, fireworks are much louder and not confined to Guy Fawkes Night. In order to be successful, preventive measures need to be taken well in advance of a likely problem situation – pre-planning and purposeful co-operation is fundamental to success.

In essence, prevention generally calls for a behaviour modification technique called systematic desensitisation. This 'tool' is used to break down the dog's anxiety by exposing him to low levels of the stimulus and rewarding him when he remains calm. The volume of the stimulus as a recording is then increased in intensity, until it is tolerated at full strength. Desensitisation has to progress at the rate that the dog's responses dictate. Slowly, slowly is the rule. Make every effort not to make a mistake by overdoing the intensity before the dog is ready. CDs of the noise of fireworks, and some other potential fear-inducing sounds, are available and these are accompanied by detailed instructions that need to be followed precisely. In case of need, consult your veterinary surgeon and/or visit www.soundsscary.com, www.fearoffireworks.com or www.companyofdogs.co.uk.

Once desensitisation has proved effective, some behaviourists recommend a process called counter conditioning. This teaches the dog that the sound he was previously phobic about actually heralds a rewarding event, such as a meal. If you have any doubt about these behaviour modification techniques, it is important to seek advice from your veterinary surgeon or a trained animal behaviourist.

One final word of warning – if a desensitised dog is not exposed occasionally to the fear-inducing sound naturally, or by playing the recorded sound on a CD, his lack of fear could become extinguished.

6. SEEKING ADDITIONAL HELP

If you have any doubt about what to do if your dog begins presenting with behavioural problems, seek advice as soon as possible. The sooner the problem is tackled, the greater the chance of success. The places to turn to are:

* The breeder of your dog
* Your veterinary surgeon
* A qualified dog behaviour specialist. Contact the Association of Behaviour Consultants (see Appendix Two), which will provide you with the name of a qualified dog behaviourist in your area. The Association for the Study of Animal Behaviour (ASAB) has launched a new scheme to certify clinical animal behaviourists within the UK. Information can be obtained from the ASAB website: www.asab.org.uk.

We cannot stress enough that your aim should always be to *prevent* inappropriate behaviour. Behaviour specialists can help in a number of cases, but their success depends very much on the owner's input and perseverance. In bad cases, particularly those involving aggression, success can be very problematical and unpredictable. Furthermore, there is often the need for several consultations, which can be costly.

CHAPTER 13

ROUTINE CARE

1. Feeding
2. Exercise
3. Grooming

From the time you bring your puppy home until the time he passes away at the end of a long and happy life, he will need regular food, exercise and grooming. He will also need regular preventative health care, including immunisation (see Chapter Fourteen) and protection against parasites (see Chapter Fifteen).

1. FEEDING

When you first bring your puppy home, he sould be fed on the same food, and in the same way, as the breeder has done since the pup was weaned. Any sudden change in diet at this stage can lead to digestive upsets. Any changes made later in life should be introduced gradually. Importantly, dogs should be provided with their own feeding bowl, and, of course, a bowl containing fresh water must be made available at all times.

TYPES OF FOOD

Dogs can thrive on a great variety of diets including:
- Commercially produced **complete** diets, presented in cans, pouches or as dry food
- Commercially produced **complementary** diets, which require supplementation with biscuit meal

- Homemade diets, comprising meat or offal, cereals, vegetables and human leftovers.

Commercially prepared dog foods from reputable companies contain all the nutrients that dogs need in the correct balance. They offer good palatability, digestibility and a suitable energy density (the dog can get enough energy without over-filling his stomach). Such diets also offer consistency, safety and convenience.

However, rather than throw away good leftover human food, such as the remains of a stew, uneaten scrambled eggs or fish (look out for bones!) it makes sense, we feel, to give small amounts of such leftovers as a supplement. Such additions, if made, should not make up more than 10 per cent of the total daily intake of food, so that the balance of nutrients is not disturbed. Dogs that have had their diet supplemented in this way have the advantage that they will always have a source of food that they will eat readily in any unexpected circumstance or emergency – but don't overdo it.

By and large we consider that the use of complete dry foods offers the best option for most dog owners. This type of food is convenient, it can be easily stored, and the exact amount required can be simply measured so that food is not wasted. Dry food can be put down for the dog to eat when he is left on his own without the risk of it 'going off' or attracting flies, and it is convenient to take on holiday or for a lengthy day trip. In contrast, canned food or food presented in a sachet, will need to be kept in a refrigerator once opened.

Despite the comments made above, the feeding of dogs comes down to personal preference. There are no hard-and-fast rules or finite rights and wrongs. Furthermore, new products are continually being offered, and the pros and cons will need to be assessed by individual dog owners. If you feel confused by the bewildering array of options, talk to your vet and your puppy's breeder. Many pet-food manufacturers offer an information service, and most provide unbiased, good-quality information. However, be aware that their own products are likely to be recommended where possible.

Whatever method you adopt, it is important to feed good-quality food, preferably from a well-respected manufacturer. Always ensure that you read the directions on the label and feed the diet in accordance with the manufacturer's instructions.

One final small word of warning – it is probably best to avoid feeding cow's milk to young puppies and only in moderation, if at all, to adult dogs, since it can cause digestive upsets.

FREQUENCY AND TIMING OF MEALS
The following regime is usually recommended.

13. FEEDING REGIMES IN RELATION TO AGE	
AGE OF PUPPY	NUMBER OF MEALS PER DAY
8-12 weeks	4
3-6 months	3
6-9 months	2
>9 months	1 or 2 as convenient

Adult dogs are best fed separately, at set times each day, preferably after the dog's main period of exercise and before you eat as a family. An ideal situation is to give your dog a small breakfast after you have eaten yourself, exercise your dog in the afternoon, groom him and give him his main meal on your return. Your dog will be full and tired, and will not be any bother to you while you eat later yourself. Finally, you should note that, with the exception of dry food, any uneaten food should be removed after it has been left down for 15-20 minutes – no longer!

SAFETY TIPS
- Make sure that you wash you dog's eating bowl carefully after each meal. Drinking bowls should be thoroughly cleaned at least once daily.
- Generally it is better not to give your dog bones to chew. Chicken bones are definitely 'out', as are cooked bones generally. This is because they can so easily become lodged in the mouth, splinter and cause damage to the mouth or digestive tract, or be crunched up and lead to constipation.
- To satisfy the dog's need to chew, to help keep his teeth clean and prevent gum disease, it is better to give your dog one of the many manufactured dog chews that are available these days.

2. EXERCISE
The amount of exercise needed by your dog is determined principally by his size (see table on page 18). However, allowances have to be made for
age and fitness. It is unkind to drag a dog that has a heart condition or arthritis on a five-mile trek! Importantly, you should make exercising your dog fun for both of you. It is not sufficient simply to let your dog loose in your garden, no matter how big an area that is, or to just walk

your dog round the block on the lead for the prescribed distance or time. However, that said, some exercise on the pavement, especially when it's wet, is useful in that it will help to keep the dog's claws worn to the right length.

The majority of the set exercise time should be spent letting your dog run free and chasing after balls and frisbees, etc. However, be careful not to overexercise your dog in very hot weather. Consider taking a bottle of water if it is very warm and sunny. You may also like to let your dog play with another dog that you trust; usually they will happily chase each other madly and play doggy games. Do not forget also to exercise your dog's mind – play hide-and-seek, for example. Use the time you take your dog for a walk to cement the relationship between you; talk to your pet about the weather, what's happening in the family, and your plans for the future – no one will hear you, except your dog!

Finally, use the exercise period to check that your dog's faeces are normal (don't forget your pooperscoop bag!) and that he urinates freely.

3. GROOMING

It is important for your relationship with your pet that you groom him regularly, preferably every day. That apart, a good brushing and combing where appropriate is good for the dog's coat and skin. Grooming also allows you to carry out a brief health check on your dog (see Chapter Eighteen).

Regular bathing of dogs is not a necessity, but is usually done by most dog owners two or three times a year. More recently, the suggestion has been made that bathing more regularly will help cement your relationship with your dog and reinforce your status. That apart, your dog may need bathing for medical reasons, because he has started to smell doggy, or because he has decided to roll in some obnoxious matter!

If it does become necessary to bath your dog, be sure to use a shampoo especially formulated for dogs and follow the maker's instructions carefully. Again, if you have any doubts, seek advice from the breeder or your veterinary surgeon.

Infestation with skin parasites is quite common these days, even in the best-run households! Some very sophisticated products are available for use on dogs and in the household both for treatment and, importantly, prevention of flea and other ectoparasite infestations. It pays to seek veterinary advice on this matter and purchase recommended, effective products. (See Chapter Fourteen.)

CHAPTER 14

IMMUNITY AND VACCINATIONS

1. Passive immunity
2. Active immunity
3. Diseases that can be prevented by vaccination
4. Vaccination regimes

All dog owners have the responsibility to do their very best to keep their pet in full health. If you are uncertain or worried about any of the matters discussed in this chapter, ask the breeder of your dog, your veterinary surgeon, or veterinary nurse for help.

1. PASSIVE IMMUNITY

Puppies have an immune system of their own at birth, but it does not become fully active until they are a few weeks old. However, they are safeguarded to some extent by protective antibodies they have adquired from their mother (so called maternally derived passive antibodies), which is known as passive immunity.

To reduce the risk of disease early in life, some such passive antibodies are passed to puppies while they are in the womb, but most come from ingesting the colostrum (first milk). Since antibodies in the colostrum can only be absorbed by puppies for the first day or so of their lives, it is obvious that pups should be encouraged to suck vigorously as soon as possible after being born. The antibodies passed to puppies in this way will give protection against all the diseases to which the mother has been exposed or been vaccinated against. On average, the level of antibodies in the puppy's blood is approximately 77 per cent of that in his mother's blood. Because maternally derived antibodies have been passively acquired, they wane quite quickly; the quantity in the blood is halved every seven to eight days. Obviously, the duration of this passive protection in an individual puppy is dependent very much on the mother's own level of protection.

A significant complicating factor is that maternally derived antibodies not only protect against disease but also prevent a proper response to vaccination. As the duration of maternally derived antibodies is determined by the level of the mother's immunity and the amount of colostrum ingested, the earliest age at which puppies will respond effectively to vaccination will vary considerably between litters and to some extent even between individuals within a litter. Much research has gone into devising vaccination regimes that will leave puppies exposed to the risk of infection for the shortest possible period of time. In other words, to reduce the so called 'immunity gap'.

More recently still, vaccines have been developed that are capable of stimulating immunity 'in the face of' low levels of maternally derived antibodies. This means that puppies can now be vaccinated by breeders at six weeks of age, before they are homed. This can be a great advantage in respect of early habituation and socialisation.

2. ACTIVE IMMUNITY

Vaccination is a complex matter. You will need to rely on veterinary advice for the best routine to adopt in your particular case, and to find out which specific vaccines are most appropriate for your needs.

As a general rule, pups are given their first injection at six to eight weeks of age and a second dose at 12 weeks. In many cases, breeders of pedigree dogs, whether they breed regularly or just occasionally raise a litter, will arrange for the puppies in the litter to be given their first dose of vaccine at six weeks of age. Prospective purchasers of puppies are advised to check that this is the case when they see the litter and choose a puppy for themselves. If the breeder does not intend to vaccinate your chosen puppy at that age, as is usually the case with crossbreed puppies, you would be wise to ask if it could be done at your expense rather than delay protection until you take the pup home. Mongrel puppies can, of course, be weaned and homed at six weeks of age, as it is only breeders registered with the Local Authority that are not allowed to sell puppies under eight weeks of age. Consult your vet about the timing of the second and possibly a subsequent dose of vaccine. He or she will know the disease situation in your area and will advise accordingly.

3. DISEASES THAT CAN BE PREVENTED BY VACCINATION

There are five serious diseases that can threaten dogs throughout their lives.

- **Canine distemper:** a viral infection that causes dogs to have runny eyes, diarrhoea, a discharge from the nose, and a severe cough. These signs are often followed by hardening of the foot pads and nervous signs, including fits, which frequently prove fatal.
- **Infectious canine hepatitis:** a highly contagious viral disease that can be fatal within as little as 24 hours, allowing no time for effective treatment. It can also cause liver and kidney damage in the long-term and may affect the eyes (hence its colloquial name 'blue eye').
- **Canine parvovirus infection:** a very serious disease that emerged in the 1970s. It can cause heart problems and pneumonia in young puppies. Older puppies and adults may experience severe vomiting and diarrhoea (often containing large amounts of blood). The disease may be rapidly fatal in very young puppies and older dogs if treatment is delayed.
- **Leptospirosis:** the two forms of leptospirosis are caused by bacteria called leptospires. Affected dogs run a high temperature, vomit severely and often become jaundiced. Those dogs that do not die acutely may suffer from chronic liver or kidney damage later in life. These infections can be passed on to people.
- **Kennel cough:** an irritating disease complex that can be caused by a number of infectious agents, including the bacterium *Bordetella bronchiseptica,* and a number of viruses, particularly canine parainfluenza virus, acting alone or in combination. This disease, although only rarely fatal, often calls for expensive, protracted treatment. Puppies and older dogs are particularly vulnerable. Kennel cough is not only picked up in kennels; any dog-to-dog contact, for example at dog shows, can result in the disease being passed on to susceptible animals.

Fortunately, effective vaccines are available to protect dogs against all the infectious diseases noted above. Their use can give pet owners and dog breeders peace of mind, as well as saving countless dogs from suffering and possible premature death. Veterinary advice is required so that the most cost-effective vaccination programme can be selected in any specific situation.

As well as the diseases mentioned above, it has recently become possible to vaccinate dogs against canine herpes virus infection and canine coronovirus infection. The former virus is one of the causes of death in young puppies (so-called 'fading puppy syndrome'), while the other virus is now considered as being responsible for a higher frequency of canine enteritis than previously realised.

4. VACCINATION REGIMES

The most commonly used multi-component vaccine (containing five routine antigens) gives protection against canine distemper, canine hepatitis, leptospirosis, canine parvovirus infection and canine parainfluenza. This is normally administered as a course of primary vaccinations, followed by annual (or as your vet advises) booster vaccinations.

PRIMARY VACCINATION

- A single injection should establish active immunity to Canine distemper, Infectious canine hepatitis and Canine parvovirus infection in dogs of ten weeks of age or older.
- Where earlier protection is required, a first dose may be given to puppies from six weeks of age. However, because maternally derived passive antibodies can interfere with the response to vaccination, a final dose at ten weeks of age or older is generally recommended.
- For an optimal response to the Parainfluenza component, and to complete immunity to Leptospirosis, animals should be vaccinated twice, two to four weeks apart, with the final vaccination at 10 weeks of age or older.

BOOSTER VACCINATIONS

- Immunity to canine distemper, infectious canine hepatitis and vanine parvovirus infection can be maintained by revaccination (boosting) at one- to three-year intervals after the primary course has been completed.
- Revaccination against canine parainfluenza virus infection is generally recommended one year after primary vaccination and subsequently before the dog is exposed to high-risk environments (such as kennelling, showing, or mixing with dogs of unknown vaccination history).
- To maintain protection against leptospirosis, a single annual booster dose is generally recommended.

The need for booster doses of vaccine, and their frequency, is a matter of some debate and controversy at this time. There is some evidence that the protection offered by primary vaccinations can last for many years, and 'boosters' may, in fact, reduce the dog's resistance. However, research has yet to be published to settle this matter once and for all. Be guided by your veterinary surgeon, who will have had access to the latest scientific information. In our opinion it makes sense not to reduce the frequency of booster vaccination too much, partly for peace of mind but also because no one wants to see the return of canine distemper or canine parvovirus infection with all the suffering those diseases can cause. It is as well to remember that vaccination has largely eliminated these diseases, and it is important not to become complacent and lower our guard.

TARGETED VACCINATIONS

Vaccines containing parainfluenza and *Brucella bronchiseptica* antigens are used to protect dogs against 'kennel cough' (see page 114). The parainfluenza antigen can be given by injection as a single antigen or as part of a multi-component vaccine, whereas the *B. bronchiseptica* antigen is given by intranasal infusion. Recently, a combined intranasal vaccine has been introduced that gives protection against parainfluenza and *B. bronchiseptica*. These vaccines are used as target vaccines to give protection at a time of need, such as before dogs are put into boarding kennels.

CHAPTER 15

PARASITES

1. Endoparasites
2. Ectoparasites
3. Parasite control for travellers

Parasites are the curse of dog owners the world over. Fortunately, there is a wide variety of products available in the fight against them, enabling us to keep our dogs happy and healthy. As with most problems involving dogs, prevention is far better than cure.

There are two groups of parasites: those that live inside the animal (called endoparasites), and those that live outside the body (called ectoparasites).

1. ENDOPARASITES
There is a large number of 'worms' or endoparasites that affect dogs in the UK, but the two most common are:
- The roundworm – *Toxocara canis*
- The tapeworm – *Dipylidium caninum*

ROUNDWORM
- *Toxocara canis* is a round, white worm, three to six inches (7-15 cms) in length.
- Currently, virtually all puppies born to bitches that have not been wormed during pregnancy will have adult worms in their intestines. They will be capable of laying eggs by the time the puppy is 21 to 30 days old.
- Puppies under three months old can be infected by eating worm eggs

found on grass, plants in the garden, or on the bitch's coat. These hatch in the puppy's stomach, moving through the body and back to the intestine, where they become adult. Very young puppies can also be infected by immature worms in their mother's milk.

- In puppies more than three months of age, the larvae make only a limited migration and lie dormant in the body tissues, particularly in the muscles, the diaphragm and kidneys.
- When bitches become pregnant, the larvae lying dormant are stimulated to migrate again. They reach the womb and the mammary glands, infecting the puppies and completing the cycle.
- Around 30 to 40 per cent of puppies less than three months of age have adult worms in their intestines, which are able to pass eggs into the environment.
- Eggs in freshly voided faeces are not infective to dogs or people. Eggs take two to three weeks to become infective.

TAPEWORM

- *D. caninum,* which lives in the small intestines of dogs, is a flat, segmented worm that can measure up to 20 inches (50 cms) in length.
- It is unusual to see a complete tapeworm shed in the faeces of infected dogs, but the individual segments, loaded with ripe eggs, are frequently seen emerging from the anus or attached to the hair under the tail. They look like grains of rice or cucumber seeds. These segments are irritant and may cause the dog to scoot along the ground on his bottom.
- Fleas are a necessary part of the life cycle of *D. caninum*. Immature flea larvae swallow the worm eggs shed by dogs and these mature into an intermediate larval stage of the worm, called a metacestode, as the flea larvae develops into an adult flea.
- When a dog kills and eats a flea containing metacestodes, the worm larvae are released in the dog's intestine and develop into adult worms.
- Prevention of infection with this tapeworm requires maintaining a regular campaign against fleas on the dog and around the home.

TREATMENT

Worm tablets can be purchased from either a chemist or from a pet shop, but it is necessary to know the type of worm infecting a dog in order to buy the correct remedy. That said, it is best to worm your puppy regularly so that you are not faced with infestation. Your puppy's breeder and your vet will be able to give you advice about regimes and products.

Sometimes, in heavy roundworm infections, live worms are vomited.

Tapeworm segments may be seen around the anus in infected dogs. However, diagnosis is often difficult, as neither of these worms cause specific signs. Tapeworms rarely cause noticeable clinical signs apart from anal irritation and digestive disturbances, but roundworm infections may be associated with poor growth, diarrhoea, or constipation, abdominal pain, possibly a pot-bellied appearance, and a decreased or increased appetite. Of course, all these signs can also be associated with other diseases.

It makes sense to speak to your vet if you are concerned. He or she may need to examine a sample of your dog's 'motions' (faeces) to find out what eggs are present so that the correct treatment can be prescribed. In the case of *D. caninum* infection, your vet will also advise you how to control fleas. In some cases involving infection with *T. canis,* you will be advised about the need to use a product that is active against migrating larvae as well as adult worms.

The elimination of the roundworm *Toxocara canis* is important because it can cause problems in people. Such cases are highlighted from time to time in the media and are often exaggerated by the anti-dog lobby. If everyone who owns a dog follows the simple advice given below, the already low risk of damage to sight, which may be associated with this infection in children, could be reduced still further and possibly even eliminated.

A recent trial has shown that there may be a link between *Toxocara canis* infection and a number of allergies found in children. Research suggests that infection with this worm can exacerbate allergic manifestations, such as asthma and eczema. This emphasises the important need for regular worming of dogs with effective products.

WORMING REGIMES

Puppies
• Puppies should be wormed regularly, as directed by a veterinary surgeon. This usually means dosing puppies for three consecutive days, at two and five weeks of age, and again before leaving for their new home. Treatment may also be required at 12 weeks of age. Thereafter, the frequency of treatment can be reduced unless the puppies remain in kennels, where re-infection occurs more readily. A newer product is available that is administered monthly from two weeks of age. Treatment is undoubtedly a complicated matter and new products are continually being developed. It is important to be guided by your veterinary surgeon.

- Puppies should be trained to defecate in a specific fenced-off area in the garden before they are taken for walks.
- Faeces from dogs less than six months old must be picked up promptly, because they may be harbouring adult worms in their intestines. Such faeces should be buried deeply or flushed down the toilet.
- Because they may be harbouring adult worms in their intestines, which are capable of shedding eggs, dogs under six months of age should not be exercised in public places where children play or where families picnic.

Adult dogs

- The frequency of dosing will depend on the product advocated by your veterinary surgeon. However, for routine control of roundworms and tapeworms, treatment at three-monthly intervals is usually recommended.

Adult bitches

- If you own a bitch, speak to your vet about controlling heat in your pet. Bitches that do not come in heat, are, like dogs, much less likely to pass on infection. Dormant larval forms can be stimulated to start migrating again during pregnancy, and also in an un-mated bitch experiencing 'false' pregnancy. As a result, the adult worms are re-established in the intestine. In entire bitches, worming during false pregnancy has been recommended.
- All bitches should be wormed during pregnancy with a product that is effective against migrating larvae. The usual regime adopted is to treat pregnant bitches daily, from day 40 of pregnancy through to two days post whelping.

ENDOPARASITE INFECTIONS FROM OVERSEAS

Now that dogs can travel to and from Europe and a number of overseas countries under the Pet Travel Scheme (PETS), there is a real risk that some endoparasitic infections, which have hitherto not been a problem in the UK, could be unwittingly introduced into this country. Some of these 'exotic' diseases of dogs are of special importance because they can also affect people – known in technical terms as 'zoonoses'.

It should be noted that PETS is designed to protect *people* in the UK, not animals. Medication prescribed under the scheme does not protect animals from tick-borne diseases because the legality is simply to treat dogs no more than 48 hours before entering or re-entering the UK.

Those blood-borne endoparastic diseases that are of particular concern are:
- Ehrlichosis
- Leishmaniasis
- Echinococcosis
- Babesiosis
- Hepatozoonosis
- Brucellosis
- Heartworm infection.

(Leishmaniasis, echinococcosis, brucellosis and heartworm can all be transmitted to people.)

Anyone intending to travel overseas with their dog is advised to consult their veterinary surgeon to obtain suitable products and advice on dosage regimes to minimise the risks of those infections. It also makes sense to seek veterinary advice concerning medication for dogs after entry or re-entry into the UK, to ensure that these new infections are properly contained. This is not something that can be tackled without professional help. Temporary isolation while medication is undertaken is a wise precaution. From the point of view of your dog's health, it is not sufficient just to follow the rules laid down by DEFRA under the Pet Travel Scheme (PETS). Any dog that falls ill after returning from an overseas visit should be taken, without delay, to a veterinary surgeon for a full clinical examination. Tests may be necessary to identify the cause of the problem and to prescribe the correct medication.

Finally, it is probably wisest not to take your pet dog overseas unless it is really necessary to do so. Just because you *can* now take your dog with you on holiday does not mean you *should*.

2. ECTOPARASITES
There are a number of ectoparasites that you will need to protect your puppy against, including fleas, lice, ticks and mites.

FLEAS
It makes sense to inspect your dog regularly for the presence of fleas. If you do find fleas (or any flea excrement, which appears as little black specks in the dog's coat), it is important to take action at once.

Fleas are one of the worst nuisances to control, and, if left to get out of control, they can rapidly take over your house and car – as well as your dog! In the case of fleas, the saying 'prevention is better than cure' has never been more appropriate.

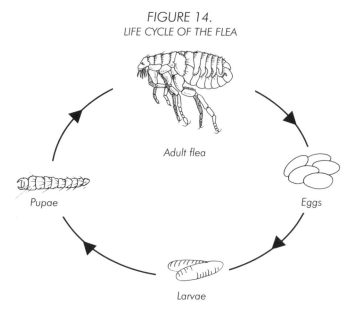

FIGURE 14.
LIFE CYCLE OF THE FLEA

Adult flea

Pupae

Eggs

Larvae

Life cycle

Adult fleas spend most of their life on their hosts. They lay eggs on the dog and subsequently fall into the environment, becoming lodged in crevices anywhere in the house, between skirting boards, carpets, and cracks between the seats and arms of upholstered chairs and car seats, etc.

The eggs develop in the environment into larvae and then into pupae. This process may take only three to four weeks in warm, humid climates, but it can take several months in the UK. The pupae lie dormant, sometimes for months. They are triggered to hatch into adult fleas by vibration in association with the right conditions of temperature and humidity.

It is important that your puppy does not become infested with fleas, because he could become sensitive to flea bites as a result. The resulting skin condition can be time-consuming and costly to cure. Indeed, in some cases, it may be possible to control the skin rash only on a temporary basis; permanent medication may be required. Flea bite dermatitis is one of the most common skin problems in dogs. Fleas can also carry the minute larvae of the common tapeworm, *Dipylidium caninum* (see page 118).

Flea control has become especially important in recent years. Many more houses now have central heating so that there are far more warm, humid places offering fleas the ideal conditions in which to multiply.

15. FLEAS: THE ESSENTIAL FACTS
• It is a myth that fleas exist only where there is dirt and disease. Central heating and carpeting provide an environment where fleas thrive.
• Fleas are armour-plated wingless insects about 2-3 mms long. They are renowned for their ability to jump huge distances for their size.
• The most common flea on dogs is the cat flea, *Ctenocephalides felis*.
• Adult fleas spend virtually all their life on their host. The intermediate stages in the flea's life cycle – larvae and pupae – develop in crevices in the house, in furnishings, between floorboards, and around the edge of fitted carpets.
• In their life-time, female fleas can lay as many as 400-500 eggs, which can be seen with the naked eye. The eggs develop into larvae and then pupae, which can remain dormant for up to a year before hatching into adult fleas.
• The presence of fleas in dogs is not the only cause of excessive scratching.
• Dogs can pick up tapeworms by swallowing fleas.
• A number of very effective products are available these days, which can be used to kill adult fleas on dogs. Other treatments have been developed that can be used very successfully in the environment, to prevent the development of eggs, larvae and pupae into adult fleas.

Diagnosis

To find out if your dog has fleas, look for small, flattened, brown, elongated wingless insects. They run over the dog's skin through the hair and jump when they are off the animal; they may be difficult to spot in dogs that groom themselves meticulously. Look particularly around the neck and at the base of the tail. If you think that fleas may be present but you can't find evidence, see your vet. Your vet will comb the dog's coat, looking for black flea dirt. These specks are about the same size as a grain of sand, and they leave a tell-tale reddish-brown mark when placed on damp blotting paper. In dogs that are hyper-sensitive to flea bites, there may be a simple papular rash on the abdomen, but, in severe cases, the skin on the back becomes thickened, folded and darkly coloured.

Treatment

Many insecticidal products are available from pet shops and chemists, but it makes sense to talk to your vet. He or she will advise whether sprays, powders, insecticidal collars, tablets, 'spot on' or injectable products are most appropriate. Be sure to seek advice on how frequently they should be used to kill existing fleas and prevent re-infection.

Prevention

A number of very effective environmental products are available for prevention of flea infestation. They contain a short-acting insecticide that will kill adult fleas, and a longer-acting compound that will prevent flea eggs from hatching and larvae from maturing into adults – breaking the whole cycle. They can give up to seven months' protection when used as directed. Your vet will advise you on the most cost-effective anti-flea campaign for your circumstances.

LICE

Trichodectes canis is transmitted by direct contact with an infected dog. Lice feed on the dog's blood, using their mouthparts to pierce the skin.

Life cycle

Adult lice feed on the skin and lay eggs on the hair. These hatch into young lice that resemble the adults. Lice cannot exist off their host for more than a few days, so infection is spread by close contacat between dogs.

Diagnosis

Light-brown, fat, wingless insects with short legs, found in the dog's coat, indicates the presence of lice. Lice move slowly on the skin surface and lay eggs (nits) that are stuck to the animal's hair, particularly around the neck and ears. Dogs with lice will scratch frequently at the area where the insects are to be found. Severe infections may cause anaemia in young puppies.

Treatment

Regular treatment of infected dogs with an insecticide is required and it makes sense to comb and wash away the nits. Since lice breed on the dog, there is less need to pay attention to the environment than is the case with flea infection.

TICKS

There are many different species of these blood-sucking insects, some indigenous to the UK and others present in overseas countries. Ticks need to be controlled because they can transmit diseases, such as ehrlichiosis, lyme disease, babesiosis and hepatozoonosis.

Life cycle

Dogs become infected by coming in contact with nymphs (young adults) or adults that have hatched from eggs laid by adult ticks. Adult ticks can be picked up by your dog when he is outside on a walk. The adults leave their natural hosts (deer, sheep and hedgehogs) and climb on to blades of grass and shrubs, waiting for a suitable host to pass, which includes dogs.

Diagnosis

Ticks are brownish-white, rounded, spider-like 'acarids'. When they are engorged with blood, they may reach the size of a bean or a pea. The adult forms lie attached to the skin by their heads, which are firmly buried in the epidermis (the outer layer of the skin). Most dogs will tolerate an adult tick or two without showing any signs. Indeed it is common for these parasites to be noticed only during routine grooming.

Treatment

Adult ticks should be removed using a proper tick-removing tool or hook available from your vet. Never attempt simply to pull the tick off your dog. You may leave the head embedded in the skin, which may lead to increased injection of toxins from the tick and/or facilitate bacterial infection into the bite. If in doubt, seek veterinary assistance. Ticks should not be handled directly.

CHEYLETIELLA MITES

Cheyletiella mites live on the skin's surface, feeding on tissue fluids. It is a non-burrowing mite.

Life cycle

These mites are just visible to the naked eye, appearing as white specks moving slowly through the skin. They lay eggs that stick to the hair. The whole life cycle, which lasts about 21 days, is spent on the host.

Diagnosis

Generally, these mites cause few signs in dogs, although heavy infections can result in marked skin scaling. The mites themselves, together with their eggs and the scurf they produce, have been called 'walking dandruff', and can be seen most frequently on the animal's back. Cheyletiella mites can cause an irritating rash in people.

Treatment

Treatment of infected dogs is relatively simple, but should be under veterinary supervision. Medication needs to be prolonged because the mite has a relatively long life cycle. One spray-on product can be used on puppies only two days of age where this is considered necessary.

MANGE MITES

There are two types of mange mite – *Demodex canis* and *Sarcoptes scabei*. Both can cause skin disease in dogs.

Demodectic mange

D. canis mites exist normally in small numbers. They live in canine hair follicles. In certain circumstances, which are not fully understood, these mites multiply dramatically and cause severe inflammation of the skin and hair loss. Usually the skin lesions are localised, but the condition may become generalised, erupting over the whole body. It can become further complicated by secondary bacterial infection. Surprisingly, dogs suffering from demodectic mange do not scratch.

The treatment of demodectic mange is controversial, but generally includes the use of insecticides administered twice weekly. Nutritional support (attention to diet) is also believed to help. Some cases eventually recover spontaneously, and the outcome (prognosis) is usually good. Dogs with the pustular form generally require long-term antibiotic therapy. The use of greasy ointments should be avoided. Treatment should be under veterinary guidance only.

Sarcoptic mange

S. scabei mites are invisible to the naked eye. They burrow superficially into the skin, causing intense irritation and frantic scratching. The areas most commonly affected are under the thighs and forelegs and the edges of the ears. Dogs of all ages and breeds may be affected. Sarcoptic mites found on dogs are contagious to people, causing a transient skin disease.

Treatment needs to be under veterinary guidance. It is complicated by the fact that the life cycle of the mite lasts about three weeks and re-infection from contaminated bedding can occur. A number of different ectoparasiticides effectively kill the mites, but their administration needs to be continued for at least four weeks. Usually, anti-inflammatory steroids are given initially, to alleviate the intense irritation. Canine scabies papules on humans usually respond promptly to topical medication, but medical advice should be sought.

GENERAL CONSIDERATIONS FOR ECTOPARASITES
Ectoparasite infection is probably the major cause of skin disease in dogs. Because the signs are not specific to any one cause, veterinary help should be sought if you suspect anything wrong.

Diagnosis

Classic signs of an ectoparasite infestation include any skin lesions or signs of skin irritation. It is vital that a proper diagnosis of the cause is made, so that the most effective treatment can be prescribed. This often involves the microscopic examination of skin scrapings. It is helpful to have to hand a good history of the case, noting details of the signs shown and their time of onset and duration, and whether they are affected by particular events, surroundings or dietary changes. Details relating to the dog's environment, particularly the bedding used and possible contact with other animals, can also help diagnosis. Finally, it is important to inform the veterinary surgeon if any person in contact with affected dogs is also showing signs of skin disease.

Treatment

Many effective anti-ectoparasitic compounds are available these days. They come in a variety of products, presented as 'spot-ons', sprays, insecticidal collars, and oral products. Although a number can be bought over the counter from chemists and pet shops, it is sensible to obtain veterinary advice, so that the most cost-effective product for your needs is chosen and the most appropriate treatment regime is followed for your circumstances.

3. PARASITE CONTOL FOR TRAVELLERS

Many parasite infections that may be encountered overseas are not, at present, endemic in the UK. Therefore, special precautions need to be taken for dogs and bitches being sent to, coming from, or returning from, foreign parts. Good preventative medication should be undertaken, coupled possibly with a short period of local isolation (quarantine). Similar precautions should be taken when dogs return home after having been in contact with animals in the UK that may have been overseas: for example, at international dog shows, such as Crufts.

DOGS GOING TO OVERSEAS COUNTRIES

If you intend to take your dog overseas, either temporarily or to stay, *always* worm him under veterinary guidance before travelling. Apply products containing long-acting ectoparasiticides, which are effective particularly against ticks. Your veterinary surgeon will be able to advise on suitable products and dosage regimes.

DOGS RETURNING FROM OVERSEAS

Under the Pets Travel Scheme (PETS) regulations, all animals returning from overseas should have been wormed and treated for ticks 24-48 hours before leaving the overseas country. However, it is sensible to isolate such animals for about seven days, and to undertake further anti-ectoparasitic and anti-endoparasitic medication under veterinary guidance. It should be noted, however, that such actions may be too late, as they will not be effective against any exotic diseases that have already been contracted. Any dog that falls ill after returning from an overseas visit, for whatever purpose, should be taken to a veterinary surgeon without delay. A full clinical examination, possibly combined with dignostic tests, will allow the problem to be identified positively and the correct medication to be prescribed.

Finally, it is worth noting that, since the introduction of PETS, the situation regarding the export of dogs to some overseas countries has changed. To find up-to-date information and complete regulations, you will need to contact DEFRA (see Appendix Two). Furthermore, some diseases that are not currently seen in the UK may become a problem in the future as a result of climate change.

EDUCATING YOUR PUPPY

Puppies are highly receptive to the world around them, and will soak up new experiences like a sponge.

MEETING THE FAMILY

The first task is to integrate your puppy with all members of the family.

Dogs and cats can learn to live in harmony, as long as their first interactions are carefully supervised.

Dogs will generally sort out their own relationship with each other, so try not to interfere too much.

Your puppy must learn to accept all animals in the family – big and small.

HANDLING AND GROOMING

If you accustom your puppy to being groomed from an early age, he will learn to accept the attention.

Handling is an important lesson to learn so that there is no such thing as 'no go' areas.

MOTIVATION AND REWARD

You can
motivate your
dog and have
fun by playing
with him.

Stroking and
verbal praise is
a big reward
for some dogs.

For other dogs,
food is the only
worthwhile
reward.

TRAINING EXERCISES

Sit is the easiest exercise to teach, and you will be rewarded with an almost instant response.

You can use a treat to lure your puppy into the Down position.

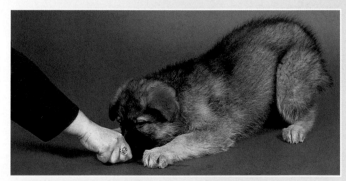

Start working on the recall exercise at an early age when your pup is keen to come to you.

The Stay
exercise needs
to be built up
as your puppy
grows in
confidence.

Lead-training
takes time and
patience.

Always end
training on a
positive note so
you can praise
your puppy.

GETTING OUT AND ABOUT

If you take your puppy out and about, he will become well socialised in all situations and will grow up to become a model member of the community.

CHAPTER 16

INHERITED CONDITIONS

1. Research
2. Breeding for good health
3. Control schemes

As a result of recent advances in veterinary medicine, 300-400 diseases and conditions in dogs have been identified as being inherited, some more common than others.

Hereditary problems may affect:
- The skeleton, including the jaw, the spine and the joints.
- The eyes, resulting in malformation and possibly blindness.
- The heart and major blood vessels, affecting structure (anatomy) and function.
- The ears, possibly resulting in deafness and anatomical defects.
- The nervous system, causing epilepsy and possibly some other nervous conditions.
- The blood, causing bleeding disorders, for example.
- The dog's temperament – resulting in behavioural abnormalities.

1. RESEARCH

Although many inherited problems have been identified, the precise mode of inheritance still needs to be established in most cases. Some conditions, such as hip dysplasia, are fairly widespread across all breeds, whereas others, such as craniomandibular osteopathy, are found in a small number of breeds only. In order to throw more light on matters of inheritance, many breed clubs are co-operating with veterinary researchers. Hopefully, this will lead to a better understanding about, and possibly the elimination of, these conditions.

2. BREEDING FOR GOOD HEALTH

Some of the more common defects seen in many breeds, and even in some crossbreeds, are:
• Umbilical or inguinal hernias
• Cleft palates
• Deformed eyelids
• Slipping patellas (kneecaps)
• Cryptorchidism (retained testicles).

These conditions can cause new owners a great deal of worry and expense. The problem may require surgical correction, and the affected dog may endure a degree of suffering. Concerned breeders are making a determined effort to prevent such problems occurring by not breeding from stock that have these conditions themselves or that have previously produced puppies with these conditions. In the breeders' code of ethics, most breed clubs state that no bitch with a known physical defect, which could be detrimental to the health and well-being of a puppy, is to be used for breeding. Also, any pedigree stock with a known hereditary fault should have a restricted registration certificate to prevent breeding.

3. CONTROL SCHEMES

Currently, there are schemes administered jointly by the British Veterinary Association and the Kennel Club aimed at eradicating hip and elbow dysplasia, and some eye conditions.

HIP DYSPLASIA
Hip dysplasia is particularly prevalent in the following popular breeds:
• German Shepherd
• Golden Retriever
• Great Dane
• Labrador
• Old English Sheepdog
• Rottweiler
• Rough Collie.

In Britain, nine different aspects of the hip are examined and graded. If your puppy belongs to a breed that has traditionally suffered from hip dysplasia, the parents should have been hip scored before being bred from. Your breeder should be able to show you the certificates with the results.

EYE CONDITIONS

The breeds most susceptible to inherited eye conditions include:
• Basset Hound
• Border Collie
• Cavalier King Charles Spaniel
• Cocker Spaniel
• Collie (Rough and Smooth)
• English Springer Spaniel
• Golden Retriever
• Irish Setter
• Labrador
• Poodle (Miniature and Toy).

There is no regulatory requirement for animals to be tested for eye disorders. Your breeder and vet will be able to tell you more about levels of risk and preventative breeding measures.

HEART PROBLEMS

Inherited heart problems quite often occur in the following breeds:
• Boxer
• Bull Terrier
• Cavalier King Charles Spaniel
• Dobermann.

Again, there is no regulatory requirement to screen for these. Good breeders will not breed from any animal with a heart condition that is known or thought to be hereditary.

DEAFNESS

It is estimated that 1 in 3,000 dogs are born deaf. Breeds commonly affected include the Dalmatian, Border Collie, and Bull Terrier. There is no genetic test for deafness susceptibility at present, but breeders have access to the BAER (brainstem auditory evoked response) test, which allows them to identify dogs free from hearing defects that can be used for breeding. Puppies may be tested at the Animal Health Trust at Newmarket from eight weeks of age.

CHAPTER 17

REPRODUCTIVE ISSUES

1. The bitch's season
2. Heat control
3. Female reproductive problems
4. Male reproductive problems
5. Castration

The reproductive system is, essentially, the only major physical difference between a dog and a bitch. While your puppy is under one year of age, you are unlikely to face problems involving the reproductive system. However, it pays to be familiar with the workings of your puppy's body and the problems/decisions you may face later in your dog's life.

1. THE BITCH'S SEASON

The onset of puberty in bitches is indicated by them 'coming on heat' or being 'in season'. The majority of bitches reach this stage when they are about six to seven months of age, but it can be as early as four months or as late as two years of age.

SIGNS AND DURATION

In most bitches, heat occurs in two stages, pro-oestrus and oestrus, each lasting about nine days. However, the duration of heat in total, and of each stage comprising it, can be very variable between animals, as well as between different heats in the same bitch.

During pro-oestrus the bitch's vulva is swollen and there is a blood-stained discharge. Although the bitch will be attractive to dogs, she does not usually allow them to mate.

In the second stage (oestrus), the vulva becomes further enlarged and turgid, while the discharge becomes straw-coloured rather than blood-stained. Characteristically, bitches will accept the male during this stage of heat.

Ovulation, the liberation of eggs from the ovaries, occurs spontaneously about two days after the onset of the second stage, i.e. about 11 days after the first signs of heat are seen.

In unmated bitches, heat is followed by a period technically referred to as metoestrus, which lasts for about 90 days. The beginning and end of this stage is not usually marked by any obvious external signs, but, as a result of the hormonal changes taking place, many bitches show signs of false pregnancy at this time.

Metoestrus is followed by a period of sexual inactivity, known as anoestrus, which lasts, on average, two to two-and-a-half months but its duration can be extremely variable.

FREQUENCY

It is principally the variation in the length of anoestrus that determines the frequency of heat in bitches. The normal interval between heats is five to 10 months; intervals of less than four months may be associated with infertility. However, breed variability can be striking. For example, German Shepherds commonly come on heat as frequently as every four to four-and-a-half months, whereas African breeds, such as the Basenji, tend to be in season only once a year. Pregnancy increases the interval to the next heat by about one month.

2. HEAT CONTROL

There are several reasons why bitch owners should control heat in their pets if they do not wish to breed from them. These are:

- To gain a health advantage. The risk of the bitch developing uterine problems, particularly pyometra, and suffering from false pregnancy or vaginal hyperplasia, is eliminated. The incidence of mammary tumours is much reduced.
- To prevent unwanted pregnancy and indiscriminate breeding.
- To make the pet more consistently companionable. A bitch's temperament can change during heat and metoestrus, especially if she suffers from false pregnancy.
- To make owning a bitch more convenient. Heat control avoids the problem of messy bleeding, unsightly vulval swelling, attractiveness to

dogs, and the need to keep the bitch confined for two to three weeks twice a year. Spayed bitches will be less inclined to stray, reducing the risk of being lost or possibly causing a road traffic accident.

Heat can be controlled by spaying (removal of the uterus) or by chemical methods. Chemical control involves using an artificial hormone similar to that contained in the human contraceptive pill. Each method has advantages and disadvantages, and the matter should be discussed, in depth, with a veterinary surgeon. It is important that you are aware of the pros and cons of each method, so that the most appropriate action can be chosen to suit your particular pet and circumstances.

It is important to realise that the choice will vary for different breeds, and will also depend on the owner's needs. Some bitches, especially in the smaller breeds, encounter few, if any, side effects following spaying. In larger breeds, however, the possibility of subsequent urinary incontinence cannot be ignored. Spayed bitches may be more inclined to put on weight in comparison with entire bitches. However, this tendency is usually quite easily controlled by decreasing the bitch's calorie intake and increasing the amount of exercise taken. Regularly weighing spayed bitches is a sensible precaution.

In some breeds a coat change may occur after the operation. Spaniels, retrievers and collies may develop a more woolly coat, while short-haired breeds, such as the Dobermann, may develop bald patches on the flanks.

If you are interested in the option of spaying, discuss the subject with your veterinary surgeon before the bitch's first season, at around five months of age. Bitches are usually spayed, provided they are healthy, at any time after their first season, but not while on heat or if they are showing signs of false pregnancy. Some vets advocate spaying before the first heat, but many others believe that it is better to let bitches experience the hormonal changes associated with at least one heat, so that they become properly mature physically and mentally.

Spaying is expensive, but it provides permanent heat control, so the costs are 'one off'. For senior citizens and people on income support, charities such as the Dogs Trust (formerly the NCDL) offer spaying at a substantially reduced cost.

3. FEMALE REPRODUCTIVE PROBLEMS

Although the conditions covered in this section are unlikely to affect bitches of less than one year of age, details are enclosed for completeness. It is hoped that they will prove to be of interest, and possibly of help as the bitch becomes older. See Appendix Three for further reading on these matters.

FALSE PREGNANCY

This is a condition in which bitches show the signs of pregnancy – nursing and lactation, for example – and yet produce no puppies, either because they have not been mated or because they have failed to conceive.

The signs of false pregnancy occur one to two months after the bitch has been on heat, and they vary greatly in type and severity. Most bitches will produce some milk and display maternal behaviour. Many will have nervous signs, including restlessness and carrying shoes and other toys around the house and taking them to their beds. A bitch that has suffered from the condition once is likely to experience it again after each subsequent heat, with the signs becoming progressively more severe.

Essentially, false pregnancy can be regarded as normal, as about 60 per cent of bitches have a false pregnancy to some degree. False pregnant bitches are capable of nursing a litter from a bitch that has died, so the condition can serve a useful purpose now in breeding kennels as it did originally in the wild.

If the signs of false pregnancy are mild, it is probably best not to give any medication or treatment. The nervous signs will disappear more quickly if the bitch is denied sympathy, and if toys and brooding objects are removed. Less milk will be produced if exercise levels are increased and the carbohydrate content of the diet reduced. It can help to limit the bitch's water intake, but access to water must not be prevented entirely.

If the signs are severe, and the above actions do not help, veterinary advice should be sought. Hormone tablets or injections help to relieve the signs, and, in some cases, bathing the mammary glands may be advised to help milk resorbtion. Sedatives may be required to control the nervous signs. Owners are often advised to have their bitch spayed if she has severe false pregnancies, since bitches that do not come on heat do not suffer from false pregnancy. The chemical control of heat, with regular hormone injections, may also help to reduce the incidence of the condition.

PYOMETRA

In this condition, there is an accumulation of large amounts of fluid in the uterus, which occurs characteristically one to two months after a bitch has been on heat. The cause is not entirely clear, but is probably brought about by an hormonal imbalance.

Typically, bitches with pyometra are very obviously ill and depressed. They drink excessively and urinate more frequently. The abdomen is often distended and the bitch may have a raised temperature. In so-called 'open' cases, there is a thick, reddish-brown, evil-smelling discharge from the vulva. There is no discharge in 'closed' cases.

The condition is more often seen in older bitches of six to seven years of age, which have not had puppies. However, that is by no means always the case. The condition has been reported in some bitches after their first heat, but this is extremely rare. The signs can be variable, so diagnosis is not always easy.

If you suspect that your bitch is suffering from this condition, it is essential to seek veterinary advice without delay. An emergency operation to remove the uterus and ovaries is usually needed to save the bitch's life. Some open cases may respond to medical treatment, and this course of action may be advised for animals in which anaesthesia and major surgery may be more risky.

MAMMARY TUMOURS

As many as 75 per cent of bitches develop mammary tumours (growths in the mammary glands) as they get older. It makes sense, therefore, to inspect the mammary glands of bitches regularly, so that any swellings can be identified early. Ideally, this should be done when the bitch is on heat and then again about a month later.

If lumps are felt, their size should be recorded and monitored carefully under veterinary supervision. The decision should then be made about the possible removal of the tumour before it has a chance to spread to other organs in the body (a situation that occurs quite often). Fortunately, many growths are not malignant and are relatively easily removed, provided that they have not been allowed to grow too large. It may be sufficient just to excise the growth itself, but sometimes one or more of the mammary glands and the associated lymph nodes may need to be removed surgically.

OTHER DISEASES AND CONDITIONS

There are a number of diseases and conditions that affect bitches specifically, such as mastitis, metritis, cystitis and eclampsia. Most affect older bitches, or occur during or after pregnancy, so they do not warrant inclusion in this text. However, they are discussed in detail in *Book of the Bitch* (see Appendix Three). However, since accidents can happen, and bitches can be mated and become pregnant at their first heat, owners of bitches should be prepared for the circumstances noted below.

Mismating/misalliance

If it is known that a bitch has been mated accidentally, especially at her first heat, veterinary help should be sought without delay. Action needs to be taken promptly, as an oestrogen injection, or the start of a course of injections, must be given within three to seven days of the mating to avert pregnancy. These injections, which are unfortunately not always effective, and may cause adverse side effects, will often cause the bitch to begin her heat all over again, and she may be even more willing to be mated on a second occasion. Adequate control measures to ensure that the bitch is not mated again will be particularly important in that situation. Recently, a product containing a compound that acts as a progesterone antagonist has been introduced. Two injections are needed 24 hours apart. They can be given from 0-45 days after mating, but early administration, before 22 days after mating, is more effective. Your veterinary surgeon will advise what course of action is most appropriate in your case.

In cases of suspected mismating, owners should be prepared to provide their veterinary surgeon with a full history of the occurrence. Sometimes, swabs are taken from the vagina to establish whether or not a mating has actually taken place. Pregnancy can be confirmed by feeling the bitch's abdomen at about 21 days after mating, and, more recently, a laboratory test has been made available that can be used to detect pregnancy from 30 days after mating. Pregnancy can also be confirmed by radiography or ultrasound scanning.

It is dangerous to the bitch's health to rely continually on averting pregnancy after mismating. Therefore, adequate preventive measures must be considered. In the case of bitches not intended for breeding, spaying (surgical removal of the uterus and ovaries under general anaesthesia) is generally the action of choice.

Unexpected pregnancy

In the case of bitches that are unexpectedly found to be pregnant, surgical removal of the ovaries and the uterus with the maturing puppies (foetuses) inside is often the action of choice. If this is not practical, or if the bitch is wanted for breeding in the future, the only option is to allow the pregnancy to proceed and whelping to take place naturally.

Think very carefully about breeding from your bitch, and if you do not want her to produce a litter, make a plan for preventing this. Apart from the need to avoid producing unwanted puppies, there is the expense of rearing a large litter properly to consider. There can be no real hope of recouping these costs with a litter of crossbreeds or mongrels.

4. MALE REPRODUCTIVE PROBLEMS

Problems with the reproductive system in young male dogs are, fortunately, quite rare, but prostate problems do affect older dogs, for example. However, there are a number of conditions that the male puppy owner should be aware of.

CRYPTORCHIDISM
The testes normally descend to the scrotum five to eight weeks after birth, although definite confirmation that a dog is cryptorchid may not be possible until the puppy is six months old. Cryptorchidism is when one (unilateral) or both (bilateral) testes fail to descend. The retained testicle has an increased chance of developing a tumour, so it should be removed surgically.

PENIS/PREPUCE PROBLEMS
Mild inflammation of the penis/prepuce, evidenced by the presence of a slight milky or coloured discharge and frequent licking of this part, is quite common. It is not normally a cause for concern, but it is best to seek veterinary advice to be sure. Bleeding from the penis is usually caused by trauma, and should receive veterinary attention as soon as possible.

An inability to protrude and retraact the penis sometwimes occurs. These cases can be associated with coitus or possibly some congenital defect. If the situation persists, veterinary help should be sought; surgical correction may be required.

TESTICULAR PROBLEMS
Orchitis (inflammation of the testes) is usually caused by an infection or possibly trauma. It is painful and requires urgent veterinary attention.

Testicular cancer is rare in young dogs, although the incidence is higher in cryptorchid dogs. Most owners first suspect something when they notice a lump in the testes or if the area is swollen. Most testicular tumours are not life-threatening, unless they have spread to other areas of the body. Vets usually advise castration if testicular tumours are present.

5. CASTRATION
Castration involves removing both testicles through a small incision at the front of the scrotal sac. The scrotum itself is left empty and the fact that the testicles have been removed is not obvious on casual observation. The operation is carried out under general anaesthetic, from which dogs usually recover rapidly. The small wound generally heals within four to six days and without complication.

Dogs are not castrated routinely to provide health advantages, as is the case with ovario-hysterectomy (spaying) in bitches. However, the operation is carried out to reduce the size of the prostate when that gland is enlarged (prostatic hypertrophy) and when tumours are present in the testes. In breeding kennels, some dogs may be castrated to render them sterile once their services are no longer required. Castration does not usually affect the dog's intelligence, playfulness or guarding ability when carried out after puberty. There is, however, a tendency for dogs to put on weight after the operation, but this can generally be controlled by reducing the dog's calorie intake and increasing the amount of exercise taken. Castration is often advocated to control hypersexual traits in dogs, such as:

• Aggression, especially towards other dogs
• Mounting other dogs, people and inanimate objects
• Territory marking, especially urination about the house
• Roaming
• Destructive behaviour
• Excitability, including excessive barking.

In male dogs, sex drive is controlled by two different mechanisms – the male sex hormone, testosterone, and parts of the cerebral cortex in the brain. The relative importance of these two systems varies considerably between individuals. As castration removes only the source of male sex hormones, it is not uniformly effective in preventing hypersexual behaviour. If the dog is mainly 'driven' by his brain, the effect of castration will be minimal. For this reason, some vets may test the likely effect of castration by blocking male hormone production using a female hormone (given by mouth or by injection).

This consideration apart, castration is usually quite helpful in controlling hypersexual behaviour. In dogs that roam, 90-100 per cent respond well following the operation. In dogs that mount other dogs, people, or inanimate objects, castration is effective in about 70 per cent of cases. In situations where dogs territory mark in the house, only about 50 per cent of dogs respond satisfactorily to castration. The effect of castration on aggression is very variable.

Castration is recommended not usually before 12 months of age, but this will vary according to your vet's opinion and your reasons for having the dog castrated. Be clear in your mind why you think your dog should be castrated, and then discuss the matter fully with your vet. He or she will be able to advise you on the best course of action, including the possibility of utilising behaviour control measures, either alone or in conjunction with the operation, to overcome a behaviour problem.

CHAPTER 18

RECOGNISING ILLNESS

1. Identifying the signs
2. Preventative health checks
3. Record-keeping

The purpose of this chapter is not to provide information on all the illnesses – including signs of illness and treatment – that your dog may suffer from. While this is the normal style in books of this nature, we feel that problems can arise from following this format.

Firstly, in the case of many common diseases, the signs are very much the same; they are not specific. Secondly, not all dogs show *all* the signs noted. This means that diagnosis can be extremely difficult for owners, making it necessary and sensible to seek help from an experienced vet, who may well need to carry out tests to confirm a tentative diagnosis. Left to their own devices, owners may try to diagnose problems for themselves, bassed on information listed in a book. While this can be beneficial in some respects (e.g. first-aid situations and mild problems), it can also result in owners reaching the wrong conclusion, leading to delayed or ineffective treatment.

In light of this problem, this chapter is structured so that it gives readers guidance on how to tell the difference betwen a dog that is simply 'off colour', a dog that has a mild illness, or a dog suffering from a serious disease or condition that requires urgent veterinary attention. Hopefully, this will lead to the earlier recognition of significant illness, more prompt treatment, and, therefore, less suffering and pain.

Our objective is to help owners to identify the signs of illness and pain in their pet, and be able to describe them accurately. This will help to build up a meaningful history of the problem, and to know if and when veterinary advice should be sought. An accurate account of your pet's illness will go a long way towards ensuring a quicker, more definitive diagnosis. It will also speed up the administration of treatment, reducing the duration of the illness, and, incidentally, the cost of treatment.

1. IDENTIFYING THE SIGNS OF ILLNESS

EARLY WARNING SIGNS
- **Changed behaviour:** By and large, dogs are creatures of habit, so any variation from a dog's normal behaviour, which is not provoked by a notable change in circumstances, may well indicate that a dog is generally unwell.
- **Inappetence:** Refusal to eat is often the first sign of illness, but it is only of real significance if it persists. Many perfectly healthy dogs will refuse to eat the occasional meal or two.
- **Raised temperature:** A dog with a raised temperature will seek a cooler place to lie. He will pant and he may feel hot to the touch. We do not advise that owners make an attempt to establish their dog's actual temperature – glass mercury thermometers can be too easily broken in the dog's rectum. Furthermore, any reading needs a degree of interpretation.
- **General weakness and lethargy:** If this is not associated with hot weather or excessive exercise, it could be an indication of some systemic disease. If signs persist for more than two to three days, an early veterinary investigation is warranted.
- **Pain:** Pain will be evidenced by crying (unprovoked vocalisation), cringing and possibly aggression. Dogs in pain will usually constantly turn and glance at the source of the pain and possibly bite at the affected area. Dogs in pain will be reluctant to leave their beds and will generally resent the site of the pain being touched.

If any of the signs noted above persist for more than two to three days, consider seeking veterinary assistance.

SPECIFIC SIGNS
- **Lameness:** Lameness may occur through pain or it may be mechanical (stiffness in a joint, for example). Lameness accompanied by a change in gait or inco-ordination may stem from a problem in the legs or

possibly the dog's back. Generally speaking, if lameness is due to pain in the foot, the leg will be carried. If the site of the pain is higher up the leg, the dog will limp. Lameness associated with significant pain calls for prompt veterinary treatment. In cases of mild lameness without pain, veterinary attention should still be sought at your earliest convenience. Acute lameness, which could have been caused by an accident, obviously calls for prompt veterinary assistance.

- **Vomiting**: Occasional vomiting (perhaps after a dog has eaten grass, for example) is of no importance. However, prolonged or persistent vomiting is significant and veterinary help should be obtained without delay. If the vomit contains blood, this is generally serious and represents an emergency – consult a vet immediately.

- **Drinking excessively:** Always pay attention to the amount of water your dog drinks daily, so that you will be able to detect any increase in thirst without delay. Obviously, dogs will drink more in hot conditions or if their food has contained larger amounts of salt than is normally the case. That apart, excessive drinking is a significant sign and may indicate kidney disease or diabetes, or, in bitches, possibly pyometra. Consult your vet promptly if your bitch starts to drink large quantities of water soon after she has been on heat. In other cases, seek veterinary help if excessive drinking continues for more than three to four days.

- **Eye discharge:** A slight or clear discharge from the eyes is quite normal, but seek veterinary advice promptly if the discharge is profuse or if it contains pus. If you suspect the discharge is associated with a wound to the surface of the eye, possibly after fighting with a cat or being knocked by the end of a lead, seek veterinary help without delay.

- **Head-shaking and scratching the ears:** This can be an early sign of ear disease (ear canker). If a discharge is coming from the ears and/or there are signs of inflammation or an unpleasant smell, make an early appointment to see your vet. If head-shaking and ear-scratching occurs suddenly, if the dog is obviously distressed and he is holding his head on one side, particularly if you have recently been in fields with long grass, seek veterinary help urgently. The dog may well have a grass seed in his ear that needs prompt removal. Never poke inside a dog's ear or try to treat ear problems with human medication. Ear canker (otitis externa) has a number of different causes and specific treatment is needed.

- **Abnormal breathing:** Rapid or difficult breathing should be regarded as an emergency. The obvious exceptions are on very hot days, following strenuous exercise, or in situations where the dog is clearly nervous. Breathing abnormalities can be associated with a number of serious conditions, such as obstructed airway or heart disease. Therefore, it is sensible to seek veterinary assistance without delay.

- **Diarrhoea:** The more frequent passage of liquid faeces (diarrhoea) is most commonly caused by digestive upsets. If you think this is the problem, withhold food for 12 hours but ensure that drinking water is freely available. When food is reinstated, offer scrambled eggs or cooked white fish, together with plain boiled rice in small quantities for a day or two. Then, gradually return to the dog's normal diet. If the diarrhoea persists, or, importantly, if the faeces contain blood, seek veterinary attention without delay.

- **Problems with passing urine:** Withholding urine may be voluntary, especially in bitches – when confined to a car or not having access to the outside, for example. In this case, the cure is obvious and there is no cause for alarm. In other situations, failing to pass urine, or straining to pass urine, is always a serious emergency and must never be neglected for more than 24 hours. Bitches may show blood in their urine when 'on heat' or after whelping, but if this happens at any other time it is a serious sign and a veterinary surgeon should be consulted as soon as possible.

- **Discharge from penis or vulva:** It is normal for bitches and dogs to clean their genitalia by licking – a small amount of discharge is no cause for concern. However, if the discharge is excessive, or if it has an obnoxious smell, veterinary help should be sought within two to three days. Bitches suffering from 'open' pyometra may pass copious amounts of blood-stained, foul-smelling discharge from the vulva. If this is suspected (shortly after the bitch has been on heat), veterinary attention is needed without any delay whatsoever (see page 143).

- **Nasal discharge:** It is normal for dogs to have a cool, moist nose. However, a warm, dry nose is not necessarily an indication that a dog is unwell. A small drop of watery mucus coming from the nostrils is quite normal, and this should simply be removed gently with a piece of damp cotton wool when the dog is groomed. However, if the discharge becomes thick, or if it contains pus or blood, seek veterinary assistance at once; there may be an injury to the nose, something may have become stuck in the nostril, or it may be an early sign of a major respiratory infection.

- **Coughing:** An occasional cough is nothing to be alarmed about, especially when it occurs after exuberant play or overenthusiastic barking. However, persistent coughing – especially if phlegm is coughed up – could indicate a lung or heart problem, and it is wise to seek veterinary attention without too much delay. Coughing is a regular sign in dogs suffering from canine distemper (although that disease is very rare these days) or kennel cough (see page 114). In the latter case, there is usually a history of the dog being kennelled recently or having been in close contact with other coughing dogs. If kennel cough is suspected, seek prompt veterinary assistance. Early treatment will mean a quicker recovery, reduced suffering, and less expense.

- **Difficulty eating:** In older dogs, this sign is often associated with tooth decay or gum disease. In younger dogs it can be associated with a foreign body lodged in the mouth (most commonly a piece of bone or a stick). If the problem persists, or if the dog shows signs of pain and distress, evidenced by continual pawing at the mouth, a prompt veterinary consultation is called for.
- **Fits, convulsions or collapse:** If a dog shows any of these signs, veterinary help must be sought as an emergency.
- **Lumps or swellings:** Lumps or swellings should be investigated by a veterinary surgeon if they do not disappear within a few days, or if they are accompanied by a raised temperature. It always makes sense to monitor the size of any swellings by comparing them with a nut, fruit or vegetable; if they are increasing significantly in size, or appear to be troubling the dog, consult your vet.

The list given above is not exhaustive. If you are particularly worried about an unusual sign shown by your dog, it is always wise to consult your veterinary surgeon without too much delay – if only to save you worry. Don't be put off because you think your vet may be too busy to be concerned with something that may appear of questionable significance. It is better to be safe than sorry and to set your mind at rest rather than have sleepless nights. After all, your dog means a lot to you and you will not want him to suffer unnecessarily.

2. PREVENTATIVE HEALTH CHECKS

A number of routine daily and weekly checks should be carried out on all dogs when they are groomed. Your dog will need, and appreciate, the attention. These checks greatly increase your chance of spotting health problems early on, saving your dog from suffering.

ALL DOGS
- The inside of the eyelids should be checked *daily* for any variation from the normal colour (in the case of jaundice, the conjunctiva will

appear yellow), inflammatory changes, and excessive or coloured discharge. At the same time, the surface of the eye (the cornea) should be examined to make sure that it is clear.

- The faeces should be checked *daily*. Note any deviations from normal in respect of colour, frequency and consistency. If any changes are seen, check the dog for other signs of illness, and think back to consider if the problem could be linked to a change in diet or something that may have been scavenged.
- The ears should be examined on a *weekly* basis to ensure that no discharge or obnoxious odour is coming from the ear canal.
- The paws need checking *weekly* for wounds, cracks and cysts between the toes. At the same time, check the claws for length and splitting, and the nail beds for any signs of excessive inflammation.
- The teeth and mouth should also be checked *monthly* for dental decay, the accumulation of tartar, and inflammation of the gums (gingivitis).
- The skin should be inspected at least *once a month* for inflammation, abrasions, hair loss, wounds and the presence of ectoparasites (see Chapter Fifteen).
- Ask your veterinary surgeon whether he would advise that you have a full veterinary check on your dog as he reaches puberty, i.e. between six and nine months of age. This could be a helpful move and give you the chance to ask about any management matters that have been troubling you. Also consider having you dog checked on a *yearly* basis by your vet – an annual MOT is no bad thing!

BITCHES

- Note *daily* the frequency, and, if possible, the colour of urine passed. More frequent 'squatting' may indicate that your bitch is about to come on heat or that she may have an impending urino-genital tract infection.
- Check *daily* how much water is being drunk. Excessive thirst may indicate impending pyometra, diabetes or a urinary tract infection.
- Look *regularly* for changes in behaviour, e.g. more frequent urination (territory marking), which may indicate that your bitch is about to come on heat, is having a false pregnancy, or may be about to fall ill.
- Look *daily* for wounds, signs of excessive licking or a discharge from the vulva. Pay particular attention at the time the bitch is on heat and for the subsequent two to three months.
- Check the bitch's mammary glands for the presence of milk by gently squeezing the teats. It is particularly important to carry out this examination after the bitch has been on heat. Check *weekly*, or even more frequently, in the subsequent two months. Feel all the mammary

glands at least *monthly* for tumours and record their size.
- Look *monthly* for thickened skin or hair loss, particularly on the elbows and hocks. Loss of hair, especially on the flanks, is often associated with some hormonal deficiencies, especially in short-coated breeds, such as the Dobermann.

DOGS
- Examine the prepuce once or twice a month for any abnormalities. A slight milky discharge is a quite normal occurrence. A severe infection of the prepuce (balanitis) is evidenced by inflammation, frequent licking and a purulent, often blood-stained discharge. Prompt medical attention is needed to prevent the condition becoming chronic.
- The testicles should be felt gently, at least monthly. Note any increased tenderness or increase/discrepancy in size. Testicular tumours are best removed surgically before they become excessively large.
- Observe the dog daily as he passes faeces. Excessive straining, especially if the faeces appear normal, may indicate that the dog has an enlarged prostate, possibly as a result of hyperplasia, inflammation, or the presence of a tumour.

3. RECORD-KEEPING
Keeping a record of the events in your dog's life is very important when it comes to prevention of disease.
Records are also helpful in enabling you to provide your vet with a more complete history should your pet fall ill. This could well save time, expense and worry, as well as saving your dog from suffering unnecessarily.

We advise that you obtain a loose-leaf note book and work out for yourself what to record. However, you should aim to include information under the following headings:
- Facts relating to your dog – name, breed, sex, home address, a photograph, any unique identification marks.
- Your veterinary surgeon's telephone number and other details relating to the practice, especially 'out of hours' service.
- Insurance details
- Record of illnesses and medication
- For bitches, a record of dates on heat and breeding
- Your dog's weight, every month for the first six months, and thereafter just four times a year.
- Details of your dog's normal daily diet.

APPENDIX 1

GLOSSARY

> 1. A-Z glossary of terms

Included in this glossary are the technical words used throughout this book as well as a number of other words that veterinary surgeons may use during a consultation. Our aim in including such a full glossary is to help improve communication between vets, nurses and pet owners, and to aid the understanding of the information given in this book.

Acute	Severe disease with a short course
Anoestrus	The period of sexual inactivity (rest) in the oestrous cycle
Antibiotic	A substance produced by micro-organisms that inhibits the growth of, or destroys, bacteria. May be given by injection, by mouth or applied locally. Many are now produced synthetically
Antigen	Any substance, such as pollen, a bacterium, or a virus, which stimulates the production of antibodies in the blood.
Associative learning	Learning by trial and error

Benign (tumour)   Slow-growing, non-malignant

BHS   Beta-haemolytic streptococci – round-shaped bacteria that may cause vaginitis and be involved as a cause of fading puppies

Body language   Postures and facial expressions used by dogs to communicate with each other

Bordetella bronchiseptica   A bacterium – one of the causes of kennel cough

Brucellosis   The disease caused by an infection with the bacterium *Brucella canis*

Canine coronovirus infection   A viral infection of dogs causing enteritis

Canine distemper   A severe viral infection of dogs not commonly seen nowadays

Canine herpes virus infection   A virus infection of dogs, a cause of fading puppies

Canker (ear)   A lay term for inflammation of the outer ear – technically called *otitis externa*

Castration   Surgical removal of the male gonads (testicles)

Classical conditioning   A form of associative learning

Colostrum   The first milk produced by the dam in the first days after giving birth, which contains protective antibodies

Congenital   Present at birth

Cryptorchidism   Failure of one or both testicles to descend into the scrotum – they are retained in the abdomen

Cutaneous   Appertaining to the skin

Cystitis   Inflammation of the urinary bladder

Defecation   The passing of faeces (excreta, motions)

Demodex canis   A dog mange mite, the cause of demodectic mange

Dew claw   An extra claw near the wrist (carpus) or below the hock. They are usually removed when puppies are a few days old

Diabetes mellitus   Lack of insulin production, leading to raised blood sugar levels

Dipylidium caninum   A tapeworm affecting dogs

Docking	Shortening the tail, carried out in young puppies – a contentious issue currently
Dys-	A prefix meaning 'painful' or 'difficult'
Ectoparasite infections	Infections caused by skin parasites, e.g. fleas, lice, mange mites
Endocrine glands	Glands that secrete hormones into the blood to act as chemical messengers, which control the function of tissues and organs in the body
Endoparasite infections	Infections caused by parasites inside the body, e.g. in the blood, intestines or respiratory system
Enteritis	Inflammation of the intestinal tract
Entire bitches	Bitches that have not been spayed (neutered)
Extinction (extinguish)	The loss of a learnt behaviour through lack of reward
Faeces	Excreta from the bowel (motions)
False pregnancy	The signs of pregnancy, nursing and lactation in non-pregnant bitches
Gingivitis	Inflammation of the gums
Habituation	To get used to (accustomed to) a stimulus
Heat	A lay term used to describe the summation of pro-oestrus and oestrus. The time when bitches are attractive to dogs and will, in the latter half, 'accept' dogs
Heredity	The process of passing traits or characteristics from one generation to the next
Hip dysplasia	Progressive inherited changes in the hip joint with the result that the joint cannot function normally
History	A description of the signs of illness, noting particularly when they occurred
Hormone	A chemical messenger produced by an endocrine gland and transported by the blood to a target organ where it will exert its effect (see also Endocrine glands)

Hyper-	A prefix meaning 'excessive'
Hyperplasia	Excessive growth (of a tissue)
Hypersexual	Oversexed
Hypertrophy	Increase in the size of an organ or tissue
Hypo-	A prefix meaning 'deficient/less than', e.g. hypothyroid – an underactive thyroid, resulting in low levels of thyroid hormone in the blood
Hypoplasia	Incomplete development of an organ or tissue e.g. vaginal hypoplasia
Hypothermia	Lowered body temperature
Hysterectomy	Surgical removal of the uterus (see also Ovariohysterectomy)
Immunity (active)	Antibodies in the blood, produced by the animal itself, stimulated by vaccination, or resulting from exposure to organisms causing disease, e.g. bacteria or viruses
Immunity (passive)	Antibodies acquired by puppies from their mothers, mostly via the first milk (colostrum), but also while the pups are in the womb
Inappetence	Reluctance or inability to eat
Inco-ordination	Lack of balance – difficulty standing and walking
Infectious canine hepatitis	A virus infection of dogs
Inguinal hernia	Protrusion of abdominal organs/contents through the inguinal canal in the groin to lie under the skin outside the abdominal muscles
Inherited	A trait or characteristic passed on from one generation to the next
Instrumental conditioning	Learning by trial and error – behaviour being determined by the result it brings
Larva (larvae _pl._)	An immature stage in the development of some parasites viz _Toxocara canis_
Leptospirosis	A bacterial disease caused by _Leptospira canicola_ (kidney disease) or _L. icterohaemorrhagiae_ (liver disease)

Lesion	A pathological change in a tissue
Lethargy	Disinclination to move
Libido	Sex drive
Lymph nodes (glands)	Glands or nodes scattered throughout the body that become swollen in the case of infection. They act as filters to remove bacteria and other debris from the blood
Malignant (tumour)	Severe, life-threatening, capable of spreading
Mammary tumours	Tumours in the mammary glands
Maternally derived passive antibodies	Antibodies in a puppy's blood stream passed on by the mother, mainly in the first milk (colostrum) but also while in the womb
Mastitis	Inflammation of the mammary glands
Metacestode	An intermediate stage in the flea's life cycle; a larval form
Metoestrus	The stage of the oestrous cycle that follows heat and precedes anoestrus
Metritis	Inflammation of the uterus
Micro-chip	A small bar-coded pellet implanted under the skin to identify dogs
Mismating	Unintentional mating. Also called misalliance or mesalliance
Motions	An alternative word for faeces – dog excrement
Mucoid	Applied to a discharge, meaning that it is like mucus
Mucus *(n)*/ **mucous** *(adj)*	A clear, slimy often tenacious fluid produced by a mucous membrane, e.g. the lining of the vagina
Myometrium	The muscles of the uterus (womb)
Neonatal	Newborn
Neutering	Removal of the male or female gonads (the testicles or ovaries)
Oestrogen	A female sex hormone produced in the ovaries by the follicles – responsible for sex drive and the female sex characteristics
Oestrus	The period during heat when the bitch will accept the male

Ovaries	The female gonads, which produce ova (eggs) and the female sex hormone oestrogen
Ovariohysterectomy	Surgical removal of the uterus and ovaries – spaying
Parvovirus infection	A serious viral infection of dogs
Passive immunity	Immunity (antibodies) acquired by a puppy from his mother, mainly through ingestion of colostrum (first milk), or, in adult dogs, by the administration of antiserum
Pathogenesis	The development of a disease process
Penis	The male copulatory organ
Perinatal	The period around the time of birth
Pheromones	A group of chemicals excreted from the external surfaces of animals that are used in communication between members of the same species. They are sometimes referred to as 'social odours' although they cannot be smelt by people. Historically, they have been used to lure insects into traps, using the pheromone produced by females to attract males. A synthetic pheromone DAP (dog appeasing pheromone) is used to calm anxious dogs
Phobia	Morbid dislike or excessive fear of a thing or situation
Poly-	A prefix meaning 'many' or 'increased'
Polydypsia	Increased thirst
Polyuria	Passing increased quantities of urine
Prepuberal	Before puberty
Prepuce	Loose skin covering the penis
Prognosis	The expected outcome of a disease
Prolapse	Protrusion, to the outside, of an abdominal organ e.g. vaginal prolapse or rectal prolapse
Proliferation	To grow in size
Pro-oestrus	The first stage of heat, when a bitch first comes 'in season' and is attractive to dogs
Prophylaxis	Prevention of a disease
Prostate gland	A gland at the base of the bladder around

	the urethra, which produces a fluid that goes to make up semen
Prostatic hypertrophy	Enlargement of the prostate gland
Puberty	The time of life when an animal becomes sexually mature
Punishment	A form of negative reinforcement. Anything that stops a behaviour because it disrupts it and ensures that it does not 'pay off'
Pupa (pupae *pl.***)**	A developmental stage of ectoparasites
Purulent	Containing pus
Pyometra	Accumulation of fluid in the uterus, usually occurring one to two months after oestrus. A serious, life-threatening condition.
Pyrexia	Raised body temperature – fever
Reinforcement	Anything that makes an animal repeat a learnt response
Sarcoptes scabei	A canine mange mite; the cause of sarcoptic mange
Season	A lay term to describe when a bitch is 'on heat'
Separation anxiety	The fear of being left alone
Socialisation	To get used to (accustomed to) different types of people and situations so that they do not invoke a fearful response
Spay (spey, spaying)	Surgical sterilisation of a female by removal of the uterus and ovaries – ovariohysterectomy
Staphylococci	Bacteria that commonly occur, particularly in association with skin disease
Stimulus	Any event, movement, sound, touch or smell detected by an animal that may generate a reaction
Streptococci	Commonly occurring bacteria that frequently affect dogs and may be associated, for example, with tonsillitis or vaginitis
Subclinical	Applied to a disease in which the signs are not obvious on clinical examination
Syndrome	A set of signs that occur together, indicating a particular condition or disease

Tartar	The accumulation of a hard deposit on the teeth
Tenesmus	Painful and ineffective straining – to pass faeces or urine
Territory marking	Urine deposited by dogs or bitches to denote their presence or to mark out their territory
Testicles	The male gonads, which produce testosterone (the male sex hormone) and spermatozoa
Testosterone	The male sex hormone responsible for male sex characteristics and libido
Toxaemia	The spread of bacterial products (toxins) in the blood from a source of infection
Toxocara canis	A roundworm affecting dogs
Transplacental	Transfer across the placenta from mother to offspring, e.g. the passage of infection or antibodies
Trauma	Injury – wounding, shock
Tumour	A growth or neoplasm
Umbilical cord	The stalk of blood vessels and tissues that join the developing foetus to the placenta
Umbilical hernia	The protrusion of an abdominal organ or contents through the umbilicus to lie under the skin outside the abdominal muscles
Umbilicus	The point on the abdominal wall where the umbilical cord emerged in the developing foetus
Undershot	Malformation of the jaw where the lower teeth protrude forwards beyond those in the upper jaw – the opposite of 'overshot'
Uterus	The womb
Vaccination	The administration of attenuated (weakened) or killed disease organisms to stimulate the production of active antibodies
Vulva	The external opening of the female genital tract
Zoonosis	A disease that is common to animals and people

APPENDIX 2

USEFUL CONTACTS

1. Dog training/ behaviour
2. Charities
3. Government
4. Kennel Club
5. Veterinary associations
6. Canine press

The following contact details may prove useful if you are trying to find out more about acquiring a puppy, overcoming problems you may have with your puppy, or if you simply want to become more involved with the 'dog world'.

1. DOG TRAINING/BEHAVIOUR

ASSOCIATION FOR THE STUDY OF ANIMAL BEHAVIOUR (ASAB)
82a High Street,
Sawston,
Cambridge,
Cambridgeshire,
CB2 4HJ.
Tel: 01223 830665
Web: http://asab.nottingham.ac.uk

ASSOCIATION OF PET BEHAVIOUR COUNSELLORS (APBC)
PO Box 46,
Worcester,

Worcestershire,
WR8 9YS.
Tel: 01386 751151
Fax: 01386 750743
Email info@apbc.org.uk
Web: www.apbc.org.uk

ASSOCIATION OF PET DOG TRAINERS
PO Box 17,
Fairford,
GL7 4WZ.
Tel: 01285 810652
Email: apdtadmin@hotmail.co.uk
Web: www.apdt.co.uk

BRITISH INSTITUTE OF PROFESSIONAL DOG TRAINERS
(BIPDT)
Bowstone Gate,
Nr. Disley,
Cheshire,
SK12 2AW.
Web: www.bipdt.net

COMPANION ANIMAL BEHAVIOUR THERAPY STUDY
GROUP (CABTSG)
The Pet Behaviour Centre,
Hillside, Upper Street,
Defford,
Worcestershire,
WR8 9AB.
Tel: 01386 750615
Email: cabtsg@btinternet.com
Web: www.cabtsg.org

COMPANY OF ANIMALS AND ANIMAL BEHAVIOUR CENTRE
Ruxbury Farm,
St. Ann's Hill Road,
Chertsey,
Surrey,
KT16 9NL.
Tel: 01932 566696 (Company of Animals)

Tel: 01932 574271 or 01932 574281 (Animal Behaviour Centre)
Email: behaviour@companyofanimals.co.uk or
office@companyofanimals.co.uk
Web: www.companyofanimals.co.uk

*THE NATIONAL ASSOCIATION OF REGISTERED PETSITTERS
(NARP)*
Priory Leasow,
Titley,
HR4 3RS.
Tel: 0870 3500 543
Email: info@dogsit.com
Web: www.dogsit.com

SOCIETY FOR COMPANION ANIMAL STUDIES (SCAS)
The Blue Cross,
Shilton Road,
Burford,
Oxfordshire,
OX18 4PF.
Tel: 01993 825597
Fax: 01993 825598
Email: info@scas.org.uk
Web: www.scas.org.uk

WEBSITES DISTRIBUTING SOUND PHOBIA CDs
www.soundscary.com
www.fearoffireworks.com
www.companyofdogs.com

2. CHARITIES

BATTERSEA DOGS HOME
4 Battersea Park Road,
London,
SW8 4AA.
Tel: 0207 622 3626
Fax: 0207 622 6451
Email: info@dogshome.org
Web: www.dogshome.org

DOGS TRUST
formerly National Canine Defence League
17 Wakley Street,
London,
EC1V 7RQ.
Tel: 020 7837 0006
Fax: 020 7833 2701
Email: info@dogstrust.org.uk
Web: www.dogstrust.org.uk

PEOPLE'S DISPENSARY FOR SICK ANIMALS (PDSA)
Whitechapel Way,
Priorslee,
Telford,
Shropshire,
TF2 9PQ.
Tel: 01952 290999
Fax: 01952 291035
Email: pr@pdsa.org.uk
Web: www.pdsa.org.uk

ROYAL SOCIETY FOR THE PREVENTION OF CRUELTY TO
ANIMALS (RSPCA)
Wilberforce Way,
Southwater,
Horsham,
West Sussex,
RH13 7WN.
Tel: 0870 333 5999
Fax: 0870 753 0048
Web: www.rspca.org.uk

THE BLUE CROSS
Shilton Road,
Burford,
Oxfordshire,
OX18 4PF.
Tel: 01993 822651
Fax: 01993 823083
Email: info@bluecross.org.uk
Web: www.bluecross.org.uk

WOOD GREEN ANIMAL SHELTER
King's Bush Farm, London Road
Godmanchester,
Cambridgeshire,
PE29 2NH.
Tel: 08701 904090
Fax: 01480 832816
Email: info@woodgreen.org.uk
Web: www.woodgreen.org.uk

3. GOVERNMENT

PET TRAVEL SCHEME – DEFRA
(Department for Environment Food and Rural Affairs)
Area 201, 1a Page Street,
London,
SW1P 4PQ.
Tel: 0870 241 1710
Fax: 020 7904 6834
Email: pets.helpline@defra.gsi.gov.uk
Web: www.defra.gov.uk/animalh/quarantine/index.htm

4. KENNEL CLUB

HEAD OFFICE
1-5 Clarges Street,
Piccadilly,
London,
W1Y 8AB.
Web: www.the-kennel-club.org.uk

SHOWS AND AWARDS
Tel: 0870 606 6750
Fax: 0207 518 1058

PETLOG (PET IDENTIFICATION SERVICE)
Tel: 0870 606 0751
Email: petlogadmin@the-kennel-club.org.uk

GENERAL ENQUIRIES
4a Alton House, Office Park,

Gatehouse Way,
Gatehouse Industrial Area,
Aylesbury,
Buckinghamshire,
HP19 8XU.
Tel: 0870 606 6750

5. VETERINARY ASSOCIATIONS

ANIMAL HEALTH TRUST
Lanwades Park,
Kentford,
Newmarket,
Suffolk,
CB8 7UU.
Tel: 08700 502424
Fax: 08700 502425
Email: info@aht.org.uk
Web: www.aht.org.uk

BRITISH SMALL ANIMAL VETERINARY ASSOCIATION
Woodrow House,
1 Telford Way,
Waterwells Business Park,
Quedgley,
Gloucestershire,
GL2 2AB.
Tel: 01452 726700
Fax: 01452 726701
Email: adminoff@bsava.com
Web: www.bsava.com

BRITISH VETERINARY ASSOCIATION
7 Mansfield Street,
London,
W1G 9NQ.
Tel: 0207 636 6541
Fax: 0207 436 2970
Email: bvahq@bva.co.uk
Web: www.bva.co.uk

BRITISH VETERINARY NURSING ASSOCIATION
Suite 11, Shenval House,
South Row,
Harlow,
Essex,
CM20 2BD.
Tel: 01279 450567
Fax: 01279 420886
Email: bvna@bvnaoffice.plus.com
Web: www.bvna.org.uk

PET HEALTH COUNCIL
1, Bedford Avenue,
London.
WC1B 3AU
Tel: 0207 255 5408
Email: phc@grayling.co.uk
Web: www.pethealthcouncil.co.uk

ROYAL COLLEGE OF VETERINARY SURGEONS
Belgravia House,
62-64 Horseferry Road,
London,
SW1P 2AF.
Tel: 0207 222 2001
Fax: 0207 222 2004
Email: admin@rcvs.org.uk
Web: www.rcvs.org.uk/

6. CANINE PRESS

DOGS TODAY
Pet Subjects Ltd,
Town Mill, Bagshot Road,
West End,
Woking,
Surrey,
GU24 8BZ.
Tel: 01276 858880
Fax: 01276 858860
Email: dogs.today@btconnect.com

DOG WORLD
Somerfield House, Wootton Road
Ashford,
Kent,
TN23 6LW.
Tel: 01233 621877
Fax: 01233 645669
Web: www.dogworld.co.uk

OUR DOGS
5 Oxford Road,
Station Approach,
Manchester,
M60 1SX.
Tel: 0870 731 6700
Fax: 0870 731 6504
Email: admin@ourdogs.co.uk
Web: www.ourdogs.co.uk

YOUR DOG
BPG (Stamford) Ltd,
33 Broad Street,
Stamford,
Lincolnshire,
PE9 1RB.
Tel: 01780 766199
Fax: 01780 754744
Email: l.leftlay@bournepublishinggroup.co.uk
Web: www.yourdog.co.uk

DOGS MONTHLY
Ascot House,
High Street,
Ascot,
Berkshire,
SL5 7JG.
Tel: 0870 730 8433
Email: acc@rtc-mail.org.uk
Web: www.corsini.co.uk/dogsmonthly

APPENDIX 3

FURTHER READING

1. Care and behaviour
2. Training and obedience
3. Activities with dogs

The information in this book covers only the first 12 months of your puppy's life. The following reading list will help you find out more about caring for your dog throughout the rest of his life, point you in the right direction should you face any problems with your dog, and give you some ideas about the many activities you can enjoy with your dog.

1. CARE AND BEHAVIOUR

ULTIMATE DOG CARE
Authors: Sue Guthrie, Dick Lane and Professor Geoffrey Summer-Smith
ISBN: 1-86054-280-8
Published by: Ringpress Books, a division of Interpet Publishing (2001)

DOGLOPAEDIA
Authors: J.M. Evans and Kay White
ISBN: 1-86054-074-0
Published by: Ringpress Books, a division of Interpet Publishing (2003)

BOOK OF THE BITCH
Authors: J.M. Evans and Kay White
ISBN: 1-86054-023-6
Published by: Ringpress Books, a division of Interpet Publishing (1997)

DO DOGS NEED SHRINKS?
Author: P. Neville
ISBN: 0-28306-041-7
Published by: Sidgwick and Jackson (1991)

PROBLEM DOG – BEHAVIOUR AND MISBEHAVIOUR
Author: Valerie O'Farrell
ISBN: 0-41318-070-0
Published by: Methuen (1994)

BSAVA MANUAL OF CANINE AND FELINE BEHAVIOURAL MEDICINE
Authors: Debra Howitz, Daniel Mills and Sarah Heath
ISBN: 0-90521-459-9
Published by: BSAVA

LIVING WITH A RESCUED DOG
Author: Julia Barnes
ISBN: 1-86054224-7
Published by: Ringpress Books, a division of Interpet Publishing (2004) in association with Dogs Trust

2. TRAINING AND OBEDIENCE

COMPETITIVE OBEDIENCE: A STEP-BY-STEP GUIDE
Author: Paddy Coughlan
ISBN 1-86054-272-7
Published by: Ringpress Books, a division of Interpet Publishing (2003)

CLICKER TRAINING FOR DOGS
Author: Karen Pryor
ISBN: 1-86054-282-4
Published by: Ringpress Books, a division of Interpet Publishing (1999)

PUPPY TRAINING THE GUIDE DOGS WAY
Author: Julia Barnes
ISBN: 1-86054-209-3
Published by: Ringpress books, a division of Interpet Publishing
(2004) in association with Guide Dogs For The Blind Association

THE PERFECT PUPPY
Author: Gwen Bailey
ISBN: 0-60058-581-6
Published by: Hamlyn, a division of Octopus Publishing Group Ltd
(1995)

THINK DOG
Author: J. Fisher
ISBN: 1-57076-250-3
Published by: Trafalgar Square Publishing (2003)

3. ACTIVITIES WITH DOGS

AGILITY: A STEP-BY-STEP GUIDE
Authors: John Gilbert and Patrick Holden
ISBN: 1-86054-044-9
Published by: Ringpress Books, a division of Interpet Publishing (2001)

DANCING WITH DOGS: A STEP-BY-STEP GUIDE
Author: Richard Curtis
ISBN: 1-860554-267-0
Published by: Ringpress Books, a division of Interpet Publishing (2003)

LIST OF
TABLES AND
DIAGRAMS

INDEX